What the L?

What the L?

25 Things We Wish We'd Known Before Going to Law School

Kelsey May
Samantha Roberts
Elizabeth Shelton

Carolina Academic Press
Durham, North Carolina

Copyright © 2010
Kelsey May
Samantha Roberts
Elizabeth Shelton
All Rights Reserved

Library of Congress Cataloging-in-Publication Data

May, Kelsey.
 What the L? : 25 things we wish we'd known before going to law school / Kelsey May, Samantha Roberts, Elizabeth Shelton.
   p. cm.
 Includes index.
 ISBN 978-1-59460-860-5 (alk. paper)
 1. Law students--United States--Handbooks, manuals, etc. I. Roberts, Samantha, 1984- II. Shelton, Elizabeth. III. Title.

KF283.M388 2010
340.071'173--dc22

2010019412

Carolina Academic Press
700 Kent Street
Durham, NC 27701
Telephone (919) 489-7486
Fax (919) 493-5668
www.cap-press.com

Printed in the United States of America

*To Annie, Molly, Rick, Vince, Jake, and Blanche,
without whom this book would never have come to fruition.
Thank you for your unwavering support and infinite snoodles.*

Contents

To L with All the Lawyers!   3
Perspectives   7

Pre L

1   A Year or Two Away and Enough Time to Play   13
2   Know Why You Go, Even if You Don't Know   17
3   Eeny, Meeny, Money, Moe   21

1L

4   What the L Is Going on Around Here?   27
5   Hello, Dolly   35
6   The 6-Week Asshole Rule   39
7   How I Met Your Mother's Nose   41
8   Professors Can Be Your BFFs, BNR (But Not Really)   45
9   How to Outline   49
10   How to *Not* Outline   53
11   4 Hours, 15 Pens, and No Clue   55
12   3.893475: Making the Grade and Rounding the Curve   61

Other Ls

13   You Want Me to Do *What*?!: Law Review   67
14   Mock Trial and Error   75
15   I See London, I See France   79
16   Why Researching in Your Underwear Might Be a Bad Idea   85
17   Wait … That Class Is at 8 a.m.? On Fridays? L No!   89
18   Find a Stranger   95
19   E-mails, Volunteering, and How to Get a Job: Oh My!   101

Post L

20	Protect Yourself by Being Professionally Active	107
21	Don't Sell Your Soul, Sell Yourself	113
22	Make It Rain	117
23	Some Lawyers Like a Small, Firm ...	125
24	A Law Student Walks into a Bar ...	129
25	3 Years of L?	135
Appendix 1	Our Unofficial Legal Dictionary	137
Appendix 2	What *Omnia* Else Means (Our Unofficial Latin Dictionary)	147
Appendix 3	Careers	151
Appendix 4	Basic Tutorial on U.S. Court Structure	157
Appendix 5	Sample Outline	159
Appendix 6	Sample Issue Map	165
Appendix 7	Sample Exam Answer	167
Acknowledgments		173

Law school means a lot of late nights, confusing assignments, and frustrating "co-counsel."

It's certainly not a small endeavor.

That's what she said.[1]

---

1. Objection—Hearsay.

What the L?

To L with All the Lawyers!

So you want to be a lawyer, huh? Congratulations! Welcome to the pursuit of justice, the epicenter of democracy, the appreciation of truth. Or something like that.

Some people go to law school and know exactly what they want to do. They know at which firm they'll work, where they'll do a clerkship, and what kind of lawyer they'll be in twenty years. We are not those people.

We are the people who went to law school for the vague reason that it will be easier to make a difference in this world with a law degree. We are the people who thought law school would be interesting in and of itself. We are the people who didn't want to get a job after college.

Law school isn't very friendly to people like us. Law school is an institution built to get a very self-motivated student into a local law firm. If that's not what you want, then you better figure it out on your own. So we've spent the last few years figuring things out ourselves. We have each approached our legal career with different backgrounds, different perspectives, and different goals. This does not make us all that different. Rather, it unifies us in the understanding that we each may have done things differently had we been equipped with the right information. While we don't have the magic key to success, we *can* share some of the things we've learned and seen, and some of the things we wish we'd been told.

The three years of law school will be simultaneously terrifying, confusing, boring, and stressful. You'll start as a 1L, so young and tender to the ways of the legal world, and progress to become a 2L, which is the year of working without any rewards. You'll soon find yourself a 3L, ditching class and desperate for a job. These L years will be transformative, and maybe even life-changing. It all starts with a single step: the application. That single step will lead you into a new world, one which you will enter and immediately think: what the L?! At least this was our experience. And three years later, we still find ourselves looking around occasionally and asking the very same question.

For a book written by three female students, you might expect a section devoted to the unique challenges of women in the legal profession, but don't look too hard—there isn't one. To be honest, we haven't really felt any of those challenges. In our experience, law school has not presented us with any major identifiable hurdles because of our gender. Sure, there's the occasional sexist comment during an interview, or the advice to wear a skirt to impress a judge, but nothing insurmountable or fundamentally offensive, at least to us. Since starting law school, we have felt essentially equal to our male peers.

However, it is mildly comforting to note that some, if not most, of the smartest people we know in law school are women, even though the most outspoken and prominent students are men. Men will likely be the editors of law review, presidents of their student bar association, and campus representatives. They will also likely be the class assholes. But they will *not* always be the smartest. Sorry, men, but it's true. If you can respect that women are as smart, and sometimes smarter, than you, you'll at least avoid the asshole category, which is all we really ask of you. And women, we're sure there's still some fighting left to do. For the women who are able to fight this fight, we are grateful. For all the others, try to mend that chip on your shoulder and approach life with a sense of humor—sometimes making enemies isn't worth it. Gender aside, this is a good generic law school lesson: the loudest, most visible students are usually not the smartest. Their visibility is most likely an attempt to compensate for a lack of something else.

We've seen a lot of things during our three years of law school—some great, some terrible. And we've learned very important lessons along the way. We have attempted to compile all of our advice into the top 25 things we wish we had known before deciding to go to law school, but we've also included feedback from professors, career counselors, and students in law schools around the country. If there's a word or phrase within these chapters that you don't know, check the dictionary in Appendix 1—it contains mostly useful definitions that you'll need in law school. Although this certainly doesn't cover everything, it should be enough to give you a good idea of what to expect and what to avoid. Armed with at least this much information, we hope the whole concept of "law school" will be much less overwhelming.

Perspectives

Kelsey

I came to law school because I wasn't ready to get a job and because I had no idea what I wanted to do. Upon entering law school, I had the idea that I would become "a lawyer," however vague that concept was. As it turns out, becoming a "lawyer" isn't quite enough. Corporate lawyer, criminal lawyer, government lawyer, tax lawyer, family lawyer, estate lawyer, appellate lawyer—as long as you live in a town with more than 500 people, there isn't really a job listing for "lawyer."

I have succeeded in law school mostly by accident and will graduate near the top of my class. Although this has the potential to sound impressive, people who make As are not that different from people who make Cs. And rest assured, not everyone in the top of the class has an easy, or even identifiable, career path. Pressure dictates that anyone with a high GPA become an associate at a large local firm directly out of law school, mainly, I'm assuming, because those are the only students who can get interviews. And while these jobs are highly coveted and have a multitude of benefits, they might not be the best option for everyone. I have learned that just because you're qualified for something does not necessarily make it right for you. Learning to say no to the wrong opportunities, at the wrong time, and yes to the right ones, at the right time, makes all the difference in the world—at least in my world. I'm still working on carving my path in the law, but it won't be traditional or pre-determined: it will be my own.

Three years (and a few breakdowns) later, I've identified the tools and lessons that would have made my ride a lot smoother. While everyone's experience is different, it helps to have an idea of what to expect and what to avoid. I hope our advice will put you at ease about the entire, terrifying experience.

Samantha

I like school. I always have. I feel obligated to disclose this from the beginning. I chose law school because I wanted to get an education that would allow me to have a substantive impact on the world in which I live—and I believe it will. I didn't come to law school with any particular passions but with many curiosities and interests, and I am leaving unaffected in that respect. With a conscious and concerted effort to step outside my comfort zone, I am graduating with much more than a pigeonholed passion in the law. I have gained far more than three additional years of formal education. And I am happy with that.

I don't know that I came to law school for the right reasons, though I certainly can't begin to demarcate between right and wrong here. Frankly, I don't think it matters. I simply wanted to further my education.

I had no ambition to be at the top of my class, and I'm not. Perhaps I can consider that a goal achieved. I didn't dream of being on law review. I had no idea what it was, and am still baffled by it. But I am confident in saying that I am a law school success and, while success is a relative term, I feel personally successful (and I venture to note that I'm an ambitious person). I don't resent my time in law school in the least, and I have found that an alarming number of people do. I loved law school. But that's because I had just enough foresight to approach it in the way that best suited me.

However, there are a few things I had to find out on my own via trial and error. Maybe figuring some things out on your own is a law school rite of passage, but I probably could have capitalized better on the opportunities available to me had I known what to look for and what to expect from the very beginning.

Elizabeth

I came to law school because I was unhappy doing menial desk work. I wanted the extra "oomph" that would help me get a job I really wanted: a job that would allow me to make a difference in people's lives, a job that would help me make a positive impact in the world, and a job I could feel good about at the end of the day. When I graduated from college, I didn't have a clear idea of what I wanted to do. I would search job listings for hours on end and turn up empty-handed. Every interesting position I found required more than I had to offer: more education, more experience, and more skills. So instead of waiting around just to get "3–5 years of experience," I decided to embrace law school and see where I ended up.

I didn't know much about law school culture before I started. I only knew that I would spend three more years going to school, and would hopefully be qualified for more interesting jobs when I finished. The first few months seemed like a blur, trying to understand law school lingo and figure out what I was "supposed" to be doing as a first year student. Thankfully, I learned that just because someone suggested that I do something did not mean it was something I had to do.

Law school presents you with choices. You can choose to study all the time, be overly outspoken in class, and network your way to law school stardom. Or, you can be like me: a law student who works hard, makes decent grades, and studies abroad because that option doesn't exist in the real world. A student who, in the end, wants to use her law degree to serve those less fortunate. I don't have any regrets about law school or the path I chose for myself. But I do have a few wish-I'd-known thoughts from my time in law school, and I hope that you will leave law school with fewer of those than me.

L PRE

1

A Year or Two Away and Enough Time to Play

Elizabeth

> "*I wish I would have taken time off before I went to law school. I feel like the more real life experience you have before law school, the more beneficial it is to you in understanding the law.*"
>
> —3L

I was out of college for two years before taking the plunge and going back to school. During that time, I applied, was accepted, freaked out, deferred, worked, and then finally enrolled. I spent plenty of hours debating—was law school right for me? Would it really help me get where I wanted to be professionally? Would I turn into a greedy, disliked "lawyer"? Was I too old?

Looking back, I realize that none of these things really mattered. Law school *was* right for me, it *did* help me in my professional life, I *don't* think I'm the punch line of a lawyer joke, and I *wasn't* too old. **Law school opens more doors than it closes** and has the potential to benefit you tremendously, despite any reservations. One of the most resounding comments we've heard from students is that they wish they hadn't gone straight from college to law school. Although plowing straight through may be the more common route, more and more students are taking time to stop and sniff the roses. And while taking time off between college and law school (either by design or accident) isn't right for everyone, it can be advantageous in a variety of ways.

Advantage 1: You Gain Work Experience

Many people don't work during their college life, but if they do, it's most often folding t-shirts in the mall or passing out burgers and fries. As a result, when graduation comes knocking and you start looking for a job, you probably don't have a lot of experience to back up the skills you claim to have. I know, I know—we are all fast learners and can learn practically anything, etc., etc. (all the ways career counselors teach you to spin it). But employers don't always buy that. I worked in college flipping burgers and serving milkshakes. When it was time to apply for professional positions, my hamburger experiences weren't quite on point.

If you take some time between college and law school, you will be able to enter the job market and acquire actual skills, which will offer a further benefit to an employer, in addition to your JD. Even if writing cover letters and interviewing seem easy, the more practice you have, the better you will be. If you go straight to law school, you may miss this first opportunity to learn what it's like to walk into a room and sell yourself. Even if it hurts your ego a bit, don't be afraid to apply for jobs and be turned down. What doesn't kill you will only make you stronger ... right?

One avenue you could take would be to spend your time before law school working in a law firm. That way you can get a taste of what the environment is like and whether that's the path you want to take. But taking time off is also a great way to explore an area that is interesting to you: the Peace Corps, teaching in a foreign country, or working for a newspaper are but a few examples. Anything is possible, and the experience will inevitably teach you more about yourself and what you want out of life. After college, I coached women's basketball at a small university, worked in a flower shop, and had a job with a non-profit organization in a large city. Not necessarily the road to professional triumph, but each job gave me a distinct perspective, and the totality of my career before law school empowered me with life experience. It also empowered me with the knowledge that my Political Science degree wasn't really going to do much for me.

Once law school starts, certain expectations are placed on you and what you will accomplish with your degree. Because of this unintended (and maybe self-imposed) pressure, you may feel more limited in what you can pursue after law school. Like working in a flower shop. Although fun, it would also be a little ludicrous ("City's Best Lawyer, Specializing in Lilies and Legal Arrangements!").

Student loans are an additional factor; if you're like me, and have taken out substantial loans, certain opportunities might not be easy to pursue after graduation. Like working in a flower shop. Although the work would be fun and the flowers pleasing to the senses, floral assistants don't get paid enough to justify $200K in student loans. These constraints influenced my decision to take the time *before* law school to explore, enjoy, and appreciate opportunities that don't require as much commitment.

One huge benefit of pre-law school work experience is the ability to pinpoint an area of the law that interests you. Most traditional law students who don't have a lot of experience won't know enough about being an attorney to know what kind of attorney they want to be. Working in a specific field may help you to know exactly what you want to do with your law degree. This, in turn, will make you more appealing to certain legal employers.

Advantage 2: You Figure Out What You Don't Want

Don't expect law school to lay out your future for you. Law school is still an educational pursuit and will present you with more options than solutions. By taking a few years to work, you will be able to learn what aspects of an office environment you like and what aspects you hate. You may even learn that you don't want to work in an office at all. Regardless, learning these preferences before going to law school will help give direction to the types of opportunities you seek for internships and a career.

From my work experience at the non-profit agency, I knew I did not want a job that would require me to be stuck behind a desk all day. This was my basis for ruling out a big firm job, at least from what I know about big firm jobs. Any employer who expects me to be in the office before the sun comes up and stay until after the sun goes down would, inevitably, become my nemesis. I love being outside; I love fresh air; and I love being able to enjoy my environment. I want to work with people, meet people, and help solve clients' problems right from the get-go. Knowing this, I haven't focused my law school career on finding a job with rigorous expectations of desk time. Instead, I'd rather use my law degree to find a job that will allow me to enjoy a little bit of free time every day and have a life away from the office. Which is why I might reconsider the florist thing.

Advantage 3: You Experience Life Without School

If you've finished twelve years of school and four years of college, the only life you've ever known is one that includes a three-month summer vacation, four weeks for winter break, endless extracurricular activities, and an enormous amount of time dedicated to homework. Life without school is much different. Depending on how you spend your time and where you live, you may have fewer friends, more free time, and no assignments to complete each night. Such independence can be exhilarating. When I started working full-time, I had to learn how to take care of myself while adjusting to a much quieter routine. I got off work at five and headed home to a grown-up house instead of going back to the dorm and hanging out with my friends all evening. It's quite an adjustment to realize that meeting new people and making new friends is a luxury of higher education, and one not always enjoyed by everyday 8–5'ers.

None of this means that traditional law students will suffer for their choice to go straight to law school. Kelsey is a "traditional" student (I think she's afraid of ever finding a real job), and she's no worse for wear. It all depends on your personal circumstances and choices. And while taking time off is not for everyone, it was the best thing for me. Take a long look at your goals, interests, financial situation, and available opportunities, and decide whether a few years of independence and soul-searching would better your chances of success in law school.

2

Know Why You Go, Even if You Don't Know

Samantha

> "I came to law school to learn the legal skills needed to pursue my ambitions of doing justice for the underprivileged."
>
> —1L
>
> "I couldn't get a job when I graduated from college. So I went to law school."
>
> —3L

"Know why you want to go to law school" might seem like the most elementary advice you've ever heard (maybe even more so than any "advice" imparted to you in *actual* elementary school). Why are *you* going to law school? It's a basic question, but the answer will help shape the next several years of your academic and professional life, not to mention alleviate the subsequent stress law school can potentially bring to your personal life. Considering your aspirations and identifying your goals before trying to achieve them will make for a much more streamlined and pleasant law school experience. **Ask yourself: why do I want to go to law school?**

First of all, there's no right answer. There's not even a conventionally "good" answer. People go to law school for so many different reasons, and no one reason is better than any other. Granted, this simple question is replete with additional underlying queries, which can be scary. If you ask yourself this question and you have a definite answer, that's a good start. If you ask yourself this question and you don't have an answer, or even an instinctive reaction, don't be alarmed—it doesn't mean that you don't know. In fact, this might even be a good sign—a sign that you are open to the opportunities that law school offers.

Here are just a few examples of how this conversation might transpire:

Scenario 1

Q: Why do I want to go to law school?

A: To become the best (fill-in-the-blank)[1] lawyer in City X.

E:[2] So maybe you know you want to be a criminal defense lawyer. Good for you. Direction is always good. You know where you want to end up and what you want to do with your law degree, so take the requisite steps to get there. This is a goal that has a clearly defined path that you'll be able to take from the beginning. Be careful with this one, though. Are you *sure* you *really* want to be a @*!# lawyer? How do you know?

Scenario 2

Q: Why do I want to go to law school?

A: Because I don't want to get a job.

E: There's not really much to say here, except that continuing to go to school will probably allow you to avoid, or even prevent you from, getting a full-time job. So this goal is pretty easy to achieve. Assuming you've been admitted to a school you don't dread and won't resent, and you have a way to finance your education, then it's easy. But if your *sole* purpose in going to law school is truly to avoid a real job, you should go to dog grooming school instead. Make sure you have at least *some* interest in the law so as to avoid a waste of time, effort, and money. Okay. Sigh of relief, you passed the first test.

---

1. Corporate, criminal defense, personal injury, etc. *Not* fill-in-the-blank with an expletive.

2. Question, Answer, Explanation.

Scenario 3

Q: Why do I want to go to law school?

A: I can't say for sure, but I want a law degree.

E: This scenario applies to about 60%[3] of law school students. You'll be in good (or at least quite a bit of) company if you think you fit in here. It's okay to not know exactly what you want to do with your legal education, but it is beneficial to *know* that you don't know ... you know? If you recognize and embrace that you don't have a clear-cut path, you can have some real academic fun. You can explore and develop your interests. You can even operate on your curiosities alone. This was my accidental approach. I didn't know what I would end up doing with my degree, and I wasn't afraid of full-time work. I just wanted to have a law degree. And I accepted this fact, which made the process much less stressful. Knowing that I was there just to *learn* and not to *be* something made the ride a lot smoother for me.

You might think my advice is superfluous. Of *course* you know why you're going to law school ... who doesn't?! A lot of people, believe it or not. And a lot of people *think* they know, even when they don't. And just because you *start* law school knowing exactly why you are there, it's fine to reevaluate on occasion. This is not a static situation where you have to decide on day one what kind of lawyer you want to be, and then you're stuck as that kind of lawyer. In fact, I don't know of anyone who has ever done that. Your attitude toward what you want from law school will change over the course of three years. That change may be dramatic, or it could be so subtle that you don't even notice. Either way, reevaluate your goals on occasion, and then get (or stay) on track.

There's a lot to be said for being in control of your own fate. Take control here. **Know why you want to get a law degree, even**

---

3. This number is completely arbitrary.

if that means acknowledging that you *don't* know exactly what you'll do with it. And know that, at the very least, you'll (theoretically) be getting smarter.

3

Eeny, Meeny, Money, Moe

Elizabeth

When selecting a law school, you will be bombarded with all kinds of information and advice. People will tell you to apply to safety schools and reach schools, and you'll be given tons of advice on how to write the perfect personal statement. While this is helpful, it's not the whole story.

I wish I had known how important it is to apply early. I had elaborate plans of getting everything ready and applying to schools in early fall (to enroll for the next year) so that my application would be on the top of the pile. This, unfortunately, did not happen. Between plan and execution, I had two major holdups, both of my own doing. First, I didn't take the LSAT during the summer or fall examination period, which would have been tremendously beneficial in assessing my chances of acceptance and getting my application packet ready early. Second, although I contacted my references in what I thought was enough time, it took *much* longer than expected for their letters of recommendation to appear on the LSAC website, and consequently, to use as part of my application materials. To make matters worse, almost all of the schools to which I applied accepted students on a rolling basis. Even though I got my applications in before the actual deadlines, the school admissions offices still received them almost three months after most other students' applications, which was about two and a half months later than I would have liked. Being at the end of the application line means fewer spots in 1L classes, and less scholarship money to go around. The later your application is reviewed means the more impressive it will need to be, which won't always (or ever) work to your advantage.

3 • EENY, MEENY, MONEY, MOE

Starting law school, I didn't have a very good idea of what I wanted to do with my degree. Everyone told me that the school I chose wouldn't matter much unless I got into one of the top five. I assumed the most important thing was that, in the end, I would have a law degree, and would thus be a more marketable candidate for any future job. My strategy was to pick cities where I wanted to live and apply to law schools there. I applied to schools based on their location because I wanted to live in a particular city for three years. What I did *not* realize is that the school's location entails much more than just three years of pleasant scenery. There are important real life consequences that arise from the very basic decision of where to attend school, geography included.

Going to law school in one state and then picking up and trying to start a legal career in another state is difficult. Not impossible, but difficult. Unless you have good contacts already established, no one in your new town will know you or have a vested interest in helping you find a job.

There is also the added complication of the bar exam. Different states have different timing and application requirements, but at some point during your law school career, maybe even as early as your 1L year, you will have to choose the state in which you want to be licensed and apply to take its bar exam. Right out of school you really only get one shot, as all bar exams will most likely be administered at the same time during the summer after your 3L year (and all bar *reviews* certainly will be). This won't pose a problem if you know where you want to end up. But if you *don't*, the default is to apply for the bar exam in the state where you attended school. And in that case, make sure you at least *somewhat* like the area where you attend law school, because you might end up staying ... out of convenience.

That was my experience with the bar application. Without a job lined up before graduation, and without a clear idea of where I wanted to work, I applied for admission to the bar in the state where I attended law school (by, you guessed it, default). Although it remains to be seen whether another state would have been a better choice, I imagine passing one bar exam is better than passing none at all.

Contrary to popular belief, not all law schools are the same. Obviously there is the issue of first tier, second tier, and so on, but even among similarly ranked schools, there are distinct differences in the experience and opportunities. Not all law schools offer the same programs, classes, or internships. A very common joint degree option at many law schools is a JD/MBA program. However, at some schools there is also the option of a JD/Masters focusing on social sciences, human rights, and tons of other subjects. But I didn't realize this until *after* I started school, which was also about the time that I realized my school did not offer any of these.

Law schools may also offer different types of clinical programs, certificates, and study abroad opportunities. All of these types of programs can make a difference in your law school experience and prospective career paths, and should be considered. Although you may not know exactly what you want to do when you graduate, or where you want to live, if you find a school that offers a clinic or other opportunity that interests you—go for it. You don't have anything to lose, and pursuing your interests never hurts.

And last but not least: money. One of the most important considerations is your financial situation. Depending on your personal circumstances, the overall price tag of your school could be critical. Consider the cost of tuition plus a significant amount for books, living expenses, and endless amounts of gourmet coffee/top-shelf liquor. Law school is expensive, and jobs are harder and harder to come by. Tuition varies drastically depending on whether the university is public or private, large or small, high-ranked or low-ranked. For most students, the cumulative cost is a huge hurdle of going to law school.

This being said, the importance of finances is wholly subjective. If you have a dream, don't let looming student loans stop you. Driven students won't need me to tell them that. But, if you're flexible (i.e., clueless) about your legal path, loans may be a more intimidating concept. Many law schools have very generous scholarship programs with some even offering full tuition scholarships.

Most full or partial tuition scholars are often subject to a minimum GPA requirement during the three years of law school. Do **not** consider this minimum GPA when weighing scholarship offers; if you can manage to get accepted and receive a scholarship, you can handle the GPA requirement. Do not let a lower minimum GPA requirement convince you that you'll be safer at one school than another.

A (free) law degree from Generic School could justifiably outweigh a law degree from Amazing School + $200,000 in student loans, depending on your overall goals. While educational funding absolutely shouldn't deter you from your dream school, leaving law school without loans will make your post-grad job search much less nerve-wracking.

Law schools are not interchangeable. Just like colleges, law schools have their own unique personalities and specialties. They also have their own scholarship programs and donors. As a future law student who is going to invest a lot of time, and probably money, into your legal education, take the time to find the school that best fits you and what you want. If you really have no idea, dust off the dartboard, tie on your blindfold, and embrace your sense of adventure.

1

4

What the L Is Going on Around Here?

Samantha

>Where are you from?
>Where'd you go to college?
>What did you get on the LSAT?
>What other schools did you get into?
>Why did you come to School X?
>What kind of law do you want to practice?

You will be asked these questions over and over and over. And over. No matter how annoying it is to be subjected to this third degree, it is even *more* disconcerting when you find that you too have resorted to this approach when talking to new classmates and potential new friends. Somehow, being tossed into this scary, overwhelming new environment makes it okay to ask moderately personal questions under the guise of small talk. But upon first meeting your new classmates, law school is the only thing you have in common—and you may not have even started yet.

Your school will inevitably have an orientation week where you will be formally introduced to your school (think library tours, career services presentations, and law school organization spiels) and to the study of law itself (think legal research, what *stare decisis* is, and a perfunctory lesson on how to read and understand a case). You might also be required to volunteer—beyond oxymoronic— at a local charity. My law school dedicated a week to getting "oriented," although that felt next to impossible at the time. I went to a few happy hours, sat through a few lectures on professionalism, and helped feed the hungry. I also met people who are still my friends to this day. Forced situations sometimes manage to breed lasting friendships after all.

You will likely find this to be true during your whirlwind of welcome-to-law-school activities too. You will do all of these things with your new classmates. And you will have the bazillion question conversation. With a bazillion new classmates. And that's okay. In fact, it really is a pretty good way to weed out, whether purposefully or naturally, those whom you may not have much in common with or may not enjoy being around.

Maybe you already know, or think you know, everyone you will be going to school with. Good for you. You're either really popular, over-eager, or delusional. But maybe you *don't* know everyone, or *anyone* for that matter. I didn't. I didn't know a single person in my new state, let alone my law school. Don't worry—your school's student organizations will offer plenty of activities for new students to meet each other and mingle with 2Ls and 3Ls. Within the first week or so, you will meet people you like—people you would be friends with outside of law school. You will also meet a lot of other people. You will likely be amazed at the depths of some of your classmates, and not in a good way. Don't let these people frustrate you; instead, just smile and know that there are normal people *somewhere* around here, even if they are sometimes hard to spot.

You can expect law school to be a strange combination of high school and college, at least socially. You shouldn't dream about arriving at the crossroads of sophistication and maturity from which genius emanates; you'll be in for a rude awakening. There will always be those people who will try to impress you with their backgrounds and ambitions: "my dad is 'it' when it comes to litigation attorneys in the entire State of X," or "I went to the University of Awe-Inspiring and majored in Magnificence," or essentially "I am going to rule the world when I get my law degree." Take it all with a grain of salt. At least one of these self-important suck-ups will be serving time in five years, which is vindication in and of itself. It's also very possible that one of these very people has *already* served time. Which is why I will reiterate: law school does not always attract the mature, intellectual crowd you might expect. Be grateful if your classmates are at least normal, because I've seen much worse.

The social calendar can be overwhelming those first few weeks. **Go to every event**, even if, or *especially* if, you still question your decision to go to law school. Go be Happy during that Hour. Even with all the weirdos, snobs, nerds, and jerks, the law school social world is fun. Be a part of it. Appreciate it. These are the stories you will tell for the rest of your life.

In addition to the jam-packed social schedule, every law school organization will be vying for your attention, money, or participation in these first few weeks. Some are fun and some are not; you'll be able to figure this out easily enough. If you want to join a legal fraternity and maintain your frat boy (or girl) status: go for it. If you want to join the Animal Rights Group and fight for dog-to-dog marriage under the Equal Pawtection Claws: go for it. It's all just for fun and a way to get involved. If you feel even *slightly* inclined to get involved: **go for it**. You won't regret it.

Academically speaking, law school is a lot different than college. Though it will partially depend on where you went to college and what your major was, law school is a completely different sort of learning environment. Many people breeze through college as a number or a nameless face. This will suddenly change when you get to law school. To put it simply, it will be hard to just show up to a law school class. Even if you were able to merely *exist* in a college course, you will have to suck it up in law school and assume an identity, which is likely to be "Ms. Lastname." And Ms. Lastname has to go to class, read for class, and pay attention. It's a wild concept.

Law school professors will typically assign reading for each class period which is to be completed before you show up to class. This reading is likely to include cases and explanatory note material, usually from an overpriced textbook. Assuming you are taking the regular, full-time 1L course load, expect to read for about 2–3 hours every night, in addition to the 4–6 hours you'll spend in class each day. If you do the math, this adds up to more hours than a full-time job. Your first semester will be time-consuming, and there's no way around it. Be prepared for a *lot* of dense reading.

You will not understand all of it and you're not expected to; that's what class is for. Read the cases and notes carefully enough to be able to discuss what you *think* they stand for, even if you're not sure. If you finish reading something and don't know why you were supposed to have read it, read it again. First-year concepts are not impossible to grasp if you take your time. **So take your time.** Second-year and third-year courses will generally require less reading and less effort, but this is something to judge for yourself when the time comes. In the beginning, work as hard as you can.

Then comes the really scary part: class. Expect assigned seating. This is one of the only ways for professors to learn names and call on people. Expect professors to call people out. This is called the Socratic Method, and it is not fun. It's a wonderfully effective and efficient approach—if you're the professor. It is wonderfully terrifying if you're the student.

Depending on the professor's style, several people may be called on during each session, either at random or in a pattern, and will be forced to summarize cases and recite their facts or answer specific questions. The biggest obstacle to get past is the I-hope-I-don't-look-like-a-moron fear. Believe me, everyone else in the class is just as scared and clueless as you. This is when a critical reading of the material really helps. If the professor believes you have at least read and attempted to understand the cases, they'll usually go pretty easy on you. If they see that you *haven't* read very thoroughly (and they can always tell), expect to look like a moron.

Back to the seating thing. If you're lucky, you'll have pre-assigned seating. If you're not, keep reading. Whether justifiably or not, law school seating arrangements tend to get competitive. Students, especially in their first year, will show up thirty minutes early to a class just to stake out their spot. The authors of this book are not thrilled with this strategy; however, if you don't want the worst seat in the room, you'll probably have to play along.

Get to class at least twenty minutes early on the first day. You might find that you can't actually enter the classroom yet as another class is finishing up, which means you might find yourself loitering in the hall, pinging on your BlackBerry (or iPhone—we're not discriminatory) in order to look busy and avoid talking to that annoying girl you quickly dismissed as lacking in friend potential during orientation week. But it's worth it. It is worth it on the first day of class, and the first day of class alone.

Where you sit on the first day of class is where you are probably going to be stuck for the rest of the semester, so make sure it is exactly where you want to sit. Though it is hard to tell someone's true character at this early juncture, try to avoid sitting next to the person who is going to talk to you in an abnormally loud voice during class. If you've noticed that a particular person is loud or extremely chatty, chances are this personality characteristic will not entirely disappear once class starts. This is the person who will talk *at* you even if you don't encourage this behavior with a response or acknowledgment. Don't be that person, and don't sit next to that person.

Unfortunately, there's only so much control you have over this. It is entirely possible you find the perfect seat, near the end of the row, next to a friend you've already made. You're feeling semicomfortable. Then the guy who drunkenly hit on you at the bar the last night of orientation sits right next to you—and pretends to never have met you before, or genuinely can't actually remember. You're stuck. And it sucks, but that's the way it works. Try to maneuver yourself so this doesn't happen.

Sometimes professors use this first day to merely inform you that they'll pass around the seating chart *next* class. This is potentially psychologically damaging news if you thought you were in the perfect spot, and you were ready to commit to that perfect spot. All that effort on your part and then no real commitment: how disappointing. In this case, you'll just have to get to class early again the next time, or at least strategize on how you can avoid sitting next to the loud-talker, annoying-girl, or obnoxious-bar-guy. This entire process is somehow really exhausting. The sooner it's over, the better.

But don't assume you're safe if you snag a seat in the back because professors are on to that trick, too. The sitting up front trick works pretty well, but it's not a sure bet. What is a sure bet: **the more you volunteer, the less you get called on** trick. If the professor takes volunteers, raise your hand for the stuff you're more comfortable with. That way, you'll likely avoid confrontation for the part of the reading that you fell asleep on top of before finishing.

We've established that you need to be prepared for class, meaning you should have critically read the assigned material *prior* to class, and be settled in a comfortable seat. You're almost there. Now it's time to actually get *through* class. One of the biggest differences between a college course and a law school course is that in law school, you are expected to learn material on your own. You are expected to read and understand the law before you ever get to class, and the professor's job is to explain and clarify. This is one of the reasons that critical reading is so important.

The almighty Socratic Method might sound scary, but if you get called on, all you really have to do is try. Say something. Say *anything*. At least anything relevant. Professors are using you as a teaching tool, so give them something to work with. Their intention is not to embarrass you in front of your classmates, although admittedly, it certainly feels like that sometimes. You'll probably find that you know what the professor is asking, or at least you'll be in the general vicinity of the correct answer. Good professors will essentially hold your hand the entire way, and each question will build off your previous answer. You'll explain the reasoning of an entire case without really having tried.

You are really at your professor's mercy. **Just do the best you can.** If you don't understand a question, it's okay to ask for some clarification. In fact, you will probably put yourself *and* the rest of the class at ease, as it's pretty painful to sit through dead silence while a student blankly stares at his textbook. You might be asked what your opinion is about something. Have an opinion, but base it on the reasoning you discussed in class; relate it to what you have discussed and avoid pontificating at length about your generalized personal views.

So that's the day-to-day stuff. Then comes the really, *really* scary part: the exam. The length of the exam will be based on the credit value of the class (a 3-credit hour class will usually culminate with a 3-hour exam, for example). Expect one exam per class. That translates to one grade per class. *That* translates to super stressful.

4 • WHAT THE L IS GOING ON AROUND HERE?

Most of your 1L exams will be primarily essay-based, but a few might have some multiple-choice questions. Always find out how the exam will be structured; it will ease your mind and will help you in knowing how to study.

Preparing for an exam is one thing. But, there is something else you need to be ready for. You won't need to *do* anything for this one, other than prepare yourself for the worst, because this can be a very unpleasant and nerve-wracking experience. So here it is, the vital piece of information that no one ever gives you: around finals time, **people will freak out**. Beyond recognition. You will become stressed out by how much *other* people are stressed out. While the best solution is to avoid these people, you really can't. Because they are *everywhere*. They will be sitting in the halls reciting their Torts outline; they will be sleeping in the library surrounded by candy wrappers; and they will be frantically calling your professors at all hours of the night. People are going to freak out. **Do not let this freak you out.** Worrying will not make you learn any quicker, and crying will not help your understanding of contract theories. The best advice we can give you about these people is to not let them get to you (easier said than done, I know). Feel free to be outright rude in your treatment of them because they won't respond to niceties in their time of crisis. The worst offenders are those who sit in the exam room ten minutes before the exam is about to start and ask everyone in the room to explain central concepts of the class to them. Or those who recite their knowledge of the subject, out loud, in the exam room before the exam officially starts. If I haven't indicated this already, I will make it clear now: **do not be one of these people.** Other people will hate you for it. And if you're not one of these people, don't feel bad about asking them to stop or leave the room. You shouldn't have to suffer more stress than absolutely necessary to pass your exam.

One student we talked to had a particularly bad exam scenario in this regard. Mr. Otherlastname's first semester Torts exam was structured in two parts, essay and multiple choice; each was timed separately so that even if a student finished the first part early, he would still have to wait to start the other part. Mr. Otherlastname finished the first section of his exam, the multiple-choice part, early. Instead of killing himself trying to review every question over and over again, Mr. Otherlastname went to grab a cup of coffee before the other part (the essay section) began. As Mr. Otherlastname was sipping his coffee, trying to breathe deeply and stay calm, Student Stressout ran up behind him. "Hey man," Student Stressout says. "What'd you put for those negligence questions? Did you understand number seven? How about that one where the guy beat up that other guy?" Mr. Otherlastname was appalled, shocked, and perturbed.

First of all, even though both students were technically on an approved break during the exam, it was still *during* the exam. Not only had the student stressed other people out *before* the exam, but he was still doing it *during* the exam! Mr. Otherlastname might not have been a law school genius, but he knew enough to know that there was potentially an ethical problem with the conversation being forced upon him, not to mention an unneeded headache. It's hard to take an exam, but it's even harder to be forced to dissect it with everyone else and compare answers when there's nothing left to be done, preparation-wise. And while his response may not have been perfect, Mr. Otherlastname made sure to get his point across to Student Stressout. Mr. Otherlastname covered his ears with his hands, hummed loudly, and swiftly walked away to take the rest of his exam in peace.

There's no good way to get ready for your first year of law school. But know that, with some effort, **you'll be fine.** Everyone is apprehensive about one aspect of law school or another, so realize you're not alone. Make some new friends, go to some semi-fun activities, and take a deep breath: the next three years are about to start.

5

Hello, Dolly

Samantha

> "*Think of law school as a job—go to work every day to be prepared for the final exam at the end.*"
>
> —Professor

Although I might update Dolly's classic to reflect the realities of the working world, one of the best practices to begin your 1L year is to treat law school like a job with working hours between 8 a.m. and 5 p.m. Maybe you came to law school so you *didn't* have to get a job and are therefore averse to the idea of treating law school like it *is* a job. But as bad as it sounds, this can be a helpful habit. You'll prepare yourself for the day when you must enter the professional workforce (that dreaded day when you realize you can't go to school forever). When it comes down to it, you'll just be taking a proactive approach to assuage the harsh realities you'll face upon graduation, passing the bar, and getting a job—realities including responsibilities to show up (on time), be prepared, and maybe even be semi-pleasant all day long. Once you get a job, your time will likely not be your own. Get used to it in law school. Be your own demanding boss. In law school, you can take steps to make a potentially rude awakening in the future a little bit more pleasant, or at least a little more bearable.[1] Your professors will explain to you no fewer than 100,000 times how "this is professional school," and you should treat it like it's a job—or at the very least,

---

1. Unless you are *extremely* disciplined, you might find yourself coasting through 3L year, and that's okay. Developing good habits during your 1L year and continuing them through your 2L year will prepare you for a real job, even if you take a break from the "8 to 5" as a 3L.

be on time, because you wouldn't dare be late to trial. Discipline yourself now so you don't have to be disciplined by someone else later.

The above advice, while arguably sensible in practice, may not be *entirely* convincing. Here's the most alluring selling point: the promise of a life outside the confines of law school. This alone might persuade you to follow the "8 to 5" rule. I found that if I put the time into my schoolwork during "normal" hours, it really wasn't necessary to read, study, or stress beyond those hours. Again, maybe this depends on your personality and what you want out of your law school education, but if you want to do well and have a well-balanced life, you can pretty much have it all … if you treat school like it is a full-time job.

People come to law school with many preexisting obligations and interests. If you are working a *real* job while in school, you probably won't be able to take this approach. If you have family obligations, you may not be able to spend all day, five days a week at school. You might acquire additional responsibilities while in law school, such as a significant time commitment to law review, mock trial, or various other law school organizations. Usually these commitments come during your 2L or 3L year, when you're able to put less time into studying and reading. I worked as a research assistant for a semester, Elizabeth worked part-time at a law firm during her 2L year, and Kelsey worked in an entirely different field for half of law school. That's fine. But if you put as much time as possible into law school during the day, you'll have much more free time on nights and weekends. You may have other things (not law-related) in your life that are important to you (and I hope you do). Law school does not have to be—and should not be—your life.

You'll find that some of your classmates have a never-ending (and exponentially growing) number of pages to read for class each week. They just have sooooo much to do! Which naturally leads a rational, well-prepared student to think: "What am I missing?" Generally, these people are either a) really dramatic, or b) telling the truth and have truly found themselves buried under ridiculous amounts of reading, writing, and arithmetic. With regard to the latter, they got themselves into that situation—no one else is responsible for it. The most likely explanation is poor time management. Once you find yourself behind, it is nothing less than overwhelming to think about trying to catch up. And for most of your classes, not having read the material at all is just not a viable option. If you don't stay caught up with your reading assignments, you'll encounter several problems, one of which will be the embarrassing moment when your professor calls on you in class and you have to say "I didn't do the reading." **Absolutely do not let this happen.** Long-term consequences of such neglect include either trying to read and learn it all at once right before the exam or never learning it at all—both of these options are bad news.

Use breaks between classes to prepare for your next class or to work on your outlines if you choose that route. It's pretty amazing what you can get done in one hour if you just sit down and do it. Know what you need to get done, when it needs to get done, and then do it. Then it's done. How's that for logic? You'll be prepared for class *and* have time to spend with your family, watch your favorite show, hang out with your friends, and run 20 miles. All in a day's work. Be efficient with your time. Because if you use your time wisely during the semester, there will be no need to become an unshaven hermit come time for final exams.

6

The 6-Week Asshole Rule

Kelsey

> "There will be a lot of assholes in your class—no way to avoid 'em."
>
> —2L

After three years, everyone in your class or section will know who the class asshole is. Everyone. Including professors, who will talk about the class asshole amongst themselves. There will be universal disdain for this person. This is the one instance where you can talk badly about someone and not have to worry if any of his friends are a part of the conversation. Because he doesn't have any.

For the first few class periods, the class asshole will be a slightly elusive creature. Since you aren't yet comfortable or familiar with the class style or content, you most likely won't be able to pinpoint what's wrong with this guy's behavior, because you will be too focused on trying to avoid looking like an asshole yourself. In these first weeks there may be imposters who masquerade themselves as assholes but turn out to not be so bad. This part is tricky because the class asshole may initially appear to be very charming. **Do not become friends with him** under any circumstances. In the event you *are* duped by this loud-mouth due to deceptive trickery and misplaced charm, you will be so closely associated with him that *you* become the class asshole without any real effort on your part.

You may be thinking that no one in law school can be *that* bad. Oh, but they can. The depths of the class asshole are astounding. This person will raise his hand during every class for no reason (I mean, he will physically speak but he will not actually *say* anything). This person will subtly mock the professor in class, to her face. This person will raise his hand to correct a professor for a misstatement. This person will go so far as to tell the professor she is wrong about the law. This person will inform the whole class that his father is an attorney so he is, naturally, a better law student than they are. This person will comment, after you ask a question, that it sounds like you are falling behind and don't understand the material; he will offer you personal tutoring sessions. This person will try to sleep with every 3L girl when he is a 1L and every 1L girl when he is a 3L. This person will lie to you about his dying grandmother/divorcing cousin/sick baby in order to gain your trust. This person will cut pages out of library books and circulate fake outlines with maliciously wrong information.

I know this sounds scary, but don't worry: *everyone* will know who the asshole in your class is. All you have to do is avoid him, do not sit next to him in a class and never associate with him in public (or private). Once you identify the asshole, do not let him frustrate you, because he will never change; just laugh with your non-asshole friends and appreciate that he makes you look better by comparison.

If halfway through the semester you can't figure out who the asshole is, then there's *really* bad news: it's you. Seek help immediately.

7

How I Met Your Mother's Nose

Samantha

> "*Professors are aware when students are doing something other than typing notes—smiling at your computer when nothing is funny is a dead give-away.*"
> —Professor

Leave your computer at home. Don't take it to class. Now, I realize this is a personal preference, at least for most classes—sometimes professors go so far as to ban laptops during class. While this might feel like some sort of an affront to your personal learning style, it's not. You will probably even thank them later for saving you from yourself. Nevertheless, you should know now that an Internet-equipped laptop could be your law school downfall.

If you are a habitual web surfer—and you know if you are—leave your computer at home. Take notes by hand, even if you type them up after class. Typing them and organizing them later will serve you well at the end of the semester, not to mention the benefits you'll reap from an occasional review of what was covered in class.

Surfing the internet distracts you, and it distracts everyone around you; games like Solitaire are just as bad, if not worse. You might think you can resist the temptation to check e-mail, poke someone on Facebook, or keep up on current events (video coverage of the balloon boy debacle of 2009, for instance, was very popular classroom entertainment—sitting in the back row was like observing an oddly silent news room of sorts, with thirty different monitors all set to breaking news).

The depths of distraction know no bounds. I've even been witness to a video chat or two. Okay, once a party. But only once. And

I don't claim full responsibility for that indiscretion, either. During our 3L fall, one of my (to remain nameless) co-authors pinged me with a video chat while I was in class and she was at home, sitting quietly at her laptop. There we were, a picture of her on my screen, and me on her screen. My computer was, of course, on mute, so it wasn't altogether distracting or interesting, except maybe to the people directly behind me—until my co-author's mother walked over to see what the fuss was about (apparently my co-author was laughing outrageously loud at my "in class and concentrating" face). Being less familiar with laptops and built-in cameras than we were, my co-author's mother attempted to find the tiny lens by getting as close as possible to the camera. So, while in class, "learning" about criminal procedure, my laptop screen went from a rather mundane shot of my co-author sitting at her kitchen table to an unfortunate close-up of a middle-aged woman's nose. This is the kind of occasion in which you will be forced to cough loudly, look down at your desk, and wipe your face in an attempt to hide the convulsions of laughter. We call this kind of occasion the "itchy lips." And *this* is one of the reasons you shouldn't take your laptop to class.

The second you check out of class—and it's inevitable—you'll find yourself reaching for entertainment, and it will be hard to check back in. You might get really bored actually *listening* to the professor, but, in the end, this is the lesser of two evils. **At least give yourself a chance to absorb what's going on.**

There have been times where I have found myself emotionally involved in what is happening on other people's computer screens. Creepy? Okay, yes. But I just can't divert my eyes when I see photos of friends of friends of friends enjoying beautiful tropical landscapes. Or when the girl in front of me, who I've never spoken to, is looking at wedding dresses and I think to myself, "Oh, that one is really pretty—I hope she picks that one." Or, "Oh no, that eye shadow is all wrong!" Because yes, you can do a virtual makeover on yourself, even while "learning" the law of property.

You can't imagine some of the things I've seen students do in class. Things far worse than video-chatting with my co-author's mother's nose. Here I will digress for a moment, because this isn't so much about computers in class, but class distractions in general, and is a worthwhile lesson nonetheless. In one of my first year courses, I actually saw, with my very own eyes, a student (in the front row!) painting her nails. Unbelievable, yes, but somehow, very sadly true.

To be fair, I can't claim to be a totally innocent bystander, or victim, of other people's indulgence in such temptations. I too am just ever so *slightly* guilty of indulging in in-class distractions, i.e., the aforementioned video chat. There are other instances, too. First year, while I was still figuring out how to approach classes, I took my computer to class honestly, albeit naively, believing that I would type my class notes while listening to the lecture.

At the time I was dealing with a brief but intense addiction to Google Earth. And, despite my good intentions, I fell off the wagon. There's no telling how many of my fellow Torts classmates accompanied me on my two-hour journey to the Great Wall of China one day.

I'm not saying it is impossible to use your computer for appropriate purposes—you should be the judge of that. And perhaps I should be able to focus better, but I can't. I've decided it is simply an unfortunate personality flaw. I'm going to loosely classify computers in class as a collective attractive nuisance of sorts—just don't quote me on that. After all, we covered that doctrine in Torts. But I was in China.

8

Professors Can Be Your BFFs, BNR (But Not Really)

Samantha

> "I wish someone had told me how important it was to get to know my professors. They are the ones who can provide you with connections and good recommendations. They're the ones who can help find you a job."
>
> —3L

Get to know your professors—it will benefit you tremendously. Keep in mind, of course, that this doesn't require you to ambush them with a barrage of questions and comments just for the sake of making yourself known. In fact, they will appreciate it if you don't. First and foremost, make a good faith effort to find the answer before asking an administrative question that's covered in the class syllabus (which you received). Do not ask: "What's the reading for Monday?" or "What time is our makeup class?" when it has been explained five times already. As one professor put it: "Don't come to me with questions that you should already know the answer to. And do *not* ask me what you missed during class on a certain day—if I could explain it that easily, we wouldn't have to have class at all."

Professors will likely tell you on the first day of class how they can be best reached outside of the classroom. For example, they typically have weekly office hours when students are welcome to stop by with questions. Take advantage of this opportunity to have one-on-one discussions. If you have a couple of friends you study with, it can be really helpful to go in to talk with a professor as a small group—at least it takes some of the pressure off you. Who knows—such dialogue might suddenly and completely illuminate your understanding of contracts. You might even find yourself discussing the latest happenings on your guilty pleasure TV shows with your professor. That's the *best*. We had a professor who would use characters from popular TV shows in her exam questions. After we finished her exams, we were more interested in piecing together the characters and where they came from than in discussing the actual substance of the questions. This probably makes us sound pretty lame, but it was one more thing we could talk to our professor about, and one more thing that made it not so intimidating.

Granted, sometimes professors don't seem so approachable. But if you have a question or need something clarified, go ask anyway. Seriously. If you're really nervous, start with an e-mail, our generation's amazingly convenient and passive-aggressive answer to almost everything. Repeat: e-mails are okay, but, please, for your sake and ours, do *not* text a professor, even if they give out their cell number. In fact, if they do offer their personal number, don't put it in your phone—a late night prank phone call from a "friend" who "borrows" your phone while you're in the bathroom could be potentially devastating. We know people who texted their professors, and we still don't get it. Understand the acceptable boundaries of professionalism and do your best to abide by them.

If your questions are met with perplexed looks or countered with questions to clarify what you just asked (that's the *worst*)— don't worry, and don't get discouraged—it happens. Here is an example of an actual exchange I had with a professor after scheduling a time before the exam to go over some questions:

> **Me:** Just to clarify, how do Legal Concept A and Legal Concept B work together in the context of a Legal Concept X Lawsuit?
>
> **Professor:** Wait, what? What are you asking me? You do know that Legal Concept A has nothing to do with Legal Concept X, right?
>
> **Me:** (long pause) I did not know that.

8 • PROFESSORS CAN BE YOUR BFFS (BUT NOT REALLY)

Sometimes nothing productive results from these exchanges except an enhanced sense of self-assurance in having tried. At the very least, the professor will know you care, which might help you if participation factors into your final grade.

Developing relationships with professors[1] will not only help facilitate your understanding of the law on a day-to-day basis, but will also prove to be an invaluable resource when applying for internships, jobs, or anything else. If a professor knows you (not necessarily just your grades or résumé), he is likely to write a more compelling letter of recommendation. Hopefully, after getting to know you, he'll feel invested in your success.

But don't go trying to make a professor your best friend just for the sake of making him your best friend. Besides, if you are looking for a best friend and your best bet is a professor, you've got bigger problems on your hands. Don't develop a relationship with a professor merely to benefit your professional development, i.e., don't look at all small talk as the means to an end (a good letter of recommendation). Maybe it makes tactical or strategic sense, but it will not go unnoticed by your professors. They, these objectively intelligent and successful professionals, will know when they see a good faith effort to learn and get involved versus a misguided attempt to get on their good side. For lack of a better term, don't be a "classhole" (class + asshole). It is transparent, disingenuous, and people will make fun of you. A lot.

Once you've succeeded in breaking down the barriers, remember to keep it in check. Keep your behavior professional in the classroom. Of course, the safe advice is to *always* keep your behavior professional, but sometimes it's worth extra emphasis. No matter how comfortable you feel with a professor, don't push the boundaries in class. When you raise your hand, don't unnecessarily and flippantly refer to things you discussed in other classes you took with that professor. It makes you look like a suck-up, which you most likely are. Don't speak up in class to attempt a joke about

---

1. Just to be clear, I mean professional relationships. If you even *considered* the kind of "relationship" that might be found in some student-teacher Lifetime movie, this chapter is of absolutely no use to you.

the death penalty. Really, Classhole … really? I have in fact witnessed this (but *not* like I was "witness" to the video chat). No one, except another Classhole, wants to be party to a classmate's painful and desperate attempt to develop rapport with a professor during class. He is not your "friend." He is your professor.

Okay, that's enough of the "don'ts": you get the picture. Do be attentive. Do ask questions. Do be professional. Do be enthusiastic. That's pretty much the "do" picture. Simple, really.[2]

I wish I'd known how enriching and fun it could be to get to know my professors; I would have made more of an effort from the very beginning. Approaching a figure of authority is, by nature, intimidating, but remember: **professors are there to help you.** It is literally their job. I tend to deliberate rather than to find definitive answers to my questions, so I had to force myself to step outside of my comfort zone. If you *don't* have those internal barriers to hurdle, then good for you—you're way ahead of where I started. But, if you *are* a little more reserved, you might have to make a conscious effort. The point is, make the effort, no matter what—even if it scares you.

---

2. It's duck soup! Yes, this phrase was new to the authors of this book, too, but it is possible you'll see it in a textbook or hear it in a lecture, as it is apparently popular among legal scholars and academics. "Duck soup" apparently means something that is easy or clear. Upon cursory Google research, its association with "easy" seems misplaced. In the real (weird pet people) world, duck soup is also a cure for ailing ferrets.

9

How to Outline

Kelsey

People in law school talk about "outlines" like they're the Holy Grail.

Do you have a good outline?
Do you want to collaborate on an outline together?
Can I borrow your outline?
Can I get an electronic copy of your outline? (These are the lazy people who didn't go to class during the semester and now want you to email them your notes. Feel free not to.)

You'll hear 2Ls and 3Ls talking about how easy a certain professor's exam is ... with a good outline. But in the first semester, no one really explains what an outline is (probably because no one really knows—you'll find this to be true with a lot of things). One of the most stressful components of 1L year is hearing so much about OUTLINES! but not knowing what they are or how to get one. The basic answer: an "outline" is a representation of the entire class in outline format, basically a very organized document containing a semester's worth of notes.

In my opinion, making and reviewing your outline is the best study tool there is; it forces you to know the information covered in the class and it helps you organize the topics in your head. This is not to say that a good outline will necessarily get you an A. Outlines will unquestionably help you on an exam, but not as much as going to class, reading the material, and asking questions.

The best outlining advice anyone can give you is that everyone does it differently, which is somehow more stressful than not knowing anything at all. But don't let other people make you nervous; you've made it this far, you'll make it through the exam. All this being said, it helps to know the basic structure of an outline.

I've made my outlines pretty much the same way from the beginning, and it has worked well for me:

> **Step 1:** Start with the class syllabus or the textbook's table of contents and make a general outline format with the big topics to be covered in the semester. Do this at the beginning of the class or within the first few weeks. With a professor who sticks to the book, I will copy the book's table of contents and recreate it in Word (in the same outline format) so I can fill it in later. Use the class syllabus as a guide for what parts of the book will be covered. You should be able to tell pretty quickly if a professor is going to remain consistent with the textbook. If she wrote it, chances are she'll follow it. For a professor who doesn't stick to the book, or doesn't even use one, she will usually give you a syllabus outlining the major topics of the semester. Use that. If neither of these applies, then an outline probably can't help you pass that class. You could ask the professor about the class structure, or maybe even more helpful, find someone who's already taken it and ask how they prepared.
>
> **Step 2:** Take really good class notes. If the professor allows computers, you can type your notes right into your outline format. If you take notes by hand, pick a day each week to type your notes under the appropriate headings in your outline. Be careful not to take too many notes. I know this sounds counterintuitive, but most of the professors I've had spend a lot of time talking without saying anything. Pay attention so you know what you have to know (it's easier than it sounds). Clean up your outline towards the end of the semester; this will enable you to see what areas you need to clarify and will also help to put the entire class in perspective. A good outline will be anywhere between 20–50 pages; keeping it on the shorter side helps.

A lot of people use handed-down outlines, especially for day-to-day class preparation. That is particularly helpful in a Socratic Method class (read: you get called on every other day), to help ensure that you're not caught (too) off guard, since you'll be able to see what's coming via the outline, but I've never used them (at least not exclusively). Something about typing up an entire semester's worth of notes and organizing them is very conducive to learning, in my experience. But, just like you always hear, it's whatever works for you; don't let other people dictate your study habits because, after all, *they* won't be taking *your* exam.

Now, here's the part where I should fess up. Yes, I think outlining for myself was beneficial and yes, I always used my own outlines. But the reason I started making my own outlines to begin with was that I had *no* idea how to *get* an outline for any of my classes. Many law students have expressed to us that they wish they would have known how to find a good, pre-made outline for any given class since making your own can be pretty time-consuming. In fact, I think the majority of students I know have never made their own outlines for this very reason.

There are plenty of websites which offer commercial outlines for sale; these are likely not worth the money. An outline is only useful if it is specific to your professor/textbook/class syllabus. Instead, brush up on your networking skills; the best way to go about finding good outlines is to make friends with 2Ls and 3Ls. Don't feel bad using any connection you have (your parents are friends, you met once at a party, you park next to each other)—they most likely did the same thing on their 1L outline hunt, too.

Most 2Ls and 3Ls will be happy to help if they can, but, if you're like me, it may be hard to approach a total stranger and ask for help. This is where law school organizations come in. The majority of legal fraternities and other social groups have a nifty resource called an "outline bank" where students have "deposited" copies (usually in some online database) of their old outlines for shared use among the organizations' members. Outline banks vary in helpfulness, but this can be a huge benefit of any law school organization. Ask about these during orientation week.

If neither of these ideas work, then, as a last resort, make friends with 1Ls who have made friends with 2Ls and 3Ls. Hopefully they'll be bold enough to ask for an outline, and hopefully they'll share with you. And if *that* doesn't work, then you're stuck with making your own outline. Or, you could try another, quite opposite, method ...

10

How to *Not* Outline

Elizabeth

I was really confused the first year of law school when everyone was abuzz about outlines. What are these things? How are they used? Why is everyone working so furiously on them ALL the time?! You now know what an outline is and how to make one (or find one). But, in addition to knowing what an outline actually is, I wish I had known that outlines aren't always as necessary as people make them out to be. Yes, it makes sense—create a document that contains *all* the information you learned over the course of the semester, bullet-point it, complain about how Word never formats it exactly how you want, and spend countless hours typing, typing, and typing, so that in the end, you have the one magical document that is going to bring you success on your exam. Whew! I'm tired just from thinking about that. It might make sense, but it's exhausting.

After my first semester, I stopped taking my computer to class, and started approaching class the old-fashioned way. I put pen to paper and began writing down what I thought was important during class. By writing it down, I couldn't just transcribe what the professor was saying—I had to listen, take it in, and decide what I was supposed to take away from the lecture and what would be helpful when studying for the exam.

I'm not a very organized person. And I'm a procrastinator. So despite the fact that I take notes in class, I don't go type them up at the end of the week or the end of the semester. I start the semester with grand plans, but I always find something more important to do when Friday or Saturday rolls around. I inevitably find myself saying, "Yeah, I'll type those up *next weekend* ... Right now I need to go walk my dog or go to that movie I've been dying to see." However, even though I go against the norm—I don't type my own outlines and I don't go scavenging for someone else's as soon as I know what my schedule is—I've managed to be okay.

Don't get me wrong—to "be okay" has taken work. I go to class, even when it's boring and dry (think Federal Income Tax). I do the assigned reading, listen, take notes, ask questions, and generally pay attention. I know, this sounds pretty basic, the type of advice you've gotten since your first day of school—but you'll be surprised at how many people *don't* do these things. **Show up to class, be prepared, and participate if called on.** Not only will this help you learn the material and be less stressed when finals begin, it will show the professor that you respect him or her. They prepare for class—why can't you? I'm not advocating raising your hand to share random comments merely for the sake of "participation," though. This is intended to encourage you to show up prepared with the assigned reading, ready to participate when the professor calls your name. My biggest pet peeve in law school was when a student was called on and said "I'll pass" because she wasn't prepared ... be prepared! It's not that hard. It was also my biggest fear that I would get called on and have to say that.

Now, if you really want to strive to be number one in your class, you probably need to put in some more effort. However, if you're like me and school is important, but not your world, you can survive without outlining and probably make some pretty decent grades along the way. The main thing you need to know is that however you decide to study—typed outline, nutshell, handwritten notes, whatever—you must figure out what works for you to learn and understand the subject you will be tested over. Just because you don't like to outline (like me) doesn't mean you will fail. It just means you may need to spend a little more time figuring out how you like to study. A good place to start? Pen and paper.

11

4 Hours, 15 Pens, and No Clue

Kelsey

> *"When exams roll around, you should be worried about preparing for the exam, not learning the law."*
> —Professor

> *"I take a 4-month break so I can bust my ass for three weeks. Finals are pretty stressful, but they're over pretty quickly."*
> —3L

> *"Cramming doesn't work in law school."*
> —Professor

> *"If you keep up with the reading, you should be fine. If you take notes on the reading, you'll be even better."*
> —2L

You will get a lot of different advice about how to take a law school exam. And since your entire grade is predicated on one exam per class per semester, they matter. Generally, first year exams are the worst; not because they're harder (although they might be), but because you've never taken one before, and you will be terrified. So yes, exams are accompanied with quite a bit of stress, but they're really not all that bad. Honestly, the best and most honest advice anyone can give you is "do what works for you," which isn't all that comforting. But there *are* some basics that everyone should know before heading into that dreaded first exam.

Your first semester, you will most likely be confronted with the choice of taking your exams on a computer or by hand. I've never taken an exam on a computer. I know this is the laptop era, many students take their computer to class, and the majority of people type their exams, but I never have. It seems easier to outline, make notes, write corrections, etc., in a bluebook versus a computer program. And I'm always scared (perhaps irrationally so) of that one technological malfunction that could potentially erase my entire exam, and thereby my entire semester. The nice thing about writing your exam is that you can't just write and write and write and write as easily as you can type; you have to think about what you want to say and in what order you want to say it. That's helpful from an organizational standpoint, and I've found one of the keys to succeeding on an exam is organization. Of course some (although not all) of the top students in the class type their exams, as does most everyone else. So it really is a preference thing. Just try to figure out early on what works for you and how you can best present information. Maybe try writing a practice exam and then typing one. Either way, if you know what you're doing, it shouldn't make a difference.

Figure out the logistics of the exam well beforehand. None of us knew that we had the option of re-scheduling an exam if it was scheduled within 24 hours of any other exam. This lack of understanding led Samantha to be an unwitting participant in her own personal "brain marathon" by taking three final exams in a three-day span. She survived without major detriment, although another person may not have. If she had known there was a process for re-scheduling her exams or paid attention to all school e-mails labeled "Exam Conflict Information," she might have taken advantage of the re-scheduling procedure. These kinds of procedural mechanisms don't feel important at the beginning of the semester, but they will become important, and you will kick yourself for not paying attention earlier.

Additionally, double-check that you take everything you will need with you to the exam itself. Seven-digit numbers were assigned to every student at our school each semester so that their exams could be graded anonymously. I cannot tell you how many times I walked into an exam room just to gasp in the panicky realization that I had absolutely no idea what my exam number was. Do not let this happen to you. The night before the exam, gather your materials together so you'll have enough time to remember if you're forgetting something.

The most helpful strategy to exam-taking is learning how to write well. Almost every student in the top of their class is an excellent (or at least above average) writer. The reason for this is simple: law school exams are often essay questions. Your ability to relate your knowledge is a central component of the exam. With a few exceptions, everyone in the class will know the law. Everyone will understand the major legal concepts. Everyone will be able to apply facts to those laws and concepts. The key to distinguishing yourself is in how you express the information and how you formulate your answer. Good writers are good test takers. This is one of the reasons practice exams are critical. Not only do they help you understand the law, the application of law to facts, and the exam style of a professor, they also help you practice writing. Do not just read practice exams and think about the answer. Do not say the answer aloud to a study partner. Write out the practice exam as if you were taking it. I know this is tedious, and it might be hard to force yourself to do, as it will require a 3–4 hour uninterrupted window of time. But do it anyway. There is no shortcut to learning how to take an exam. Professors have told us that their most important piece of advice for a 1L is to **take practice exams.** They go out of their way to make old exams available to you, and there's a reason for that. Who knows, you might even get lucky and see a repeat issue on the latest exam. Not probable, but possible.

On the traditional law school exam (which your first year exams are bound to be), you'll get a really long fact pattern (usually about a page) with several major issues and a few minor ones tossed in. While it's *always* a good idea to outline your answer first, and I would highly recommend it to people who aren't yet comfortable with their writing style (especially for 1L classes like Torts and Contracts), I must admit I don't always do this. But I do format my essay into somewhat of an outline form. Even if you don't have a formal outline before you start writing, make sure you have at least identified what the legal issues are—you don't have to know how the analysis for each issue will conclude before you start, but know the major topics you need to discuss, and come up with a rational order for discussing them. It is especially helpful to mark up the fact pattern itself. You should circle the major facts and other clues a professor has included. Look for key words and dramatic factual situations. You will be able to organize your exam into the broader categories of certain claims/causes of action/issues, and then use each of those sections to describe the relevant standards and legal tests that relate to that issue.

Always remember to write in essay form with complete sentences, even if you add headings and subheadings. The best technique is to write with your specific professor in mind; learn his style, the way he writes, speaks, and acts, and try to emulate that. If you can learn to get your point across in the same way your professor does, it will work wonders. Like almost everything else, this isn't as hard as it seems. Read his e-mails, class syllabus, and previous exam questions. If you pay attention, you should pick it up without too much trouble.

Another key factor in exam-taking is to remember (and **use**) the exact set of facts you are given. Professors write every sentence in their exam for a reason, and what they *don't* want to see is you assuming facts or ignoring facts. It might be easier to apply the law to a set of facts you're already familiar with, but that would defeat the purpose of an exam. **Never** ignore facts; you'll not only miss a few issues, but you might even insult your professor by leaving out juicy parts of his exam.

Start with a broad introduction of the entire essay and a brief overview of the issues you see (in a torts exam, for example, something about how unlucky the plaintiff is, what a long legal road she has in front of her, etc.—it helps to be somewhat clever and casual, but not snarky or conceited). Then, label your topics before analyzing them. You can either organize your essay by the chronological chain of events in the fact pattern or by causes of action, whichever fits better with the class and exam. So, in a torts exam, your essay exam would look something like this:

> *Tina Plaintiff certainly has had an unfortunate turn of events lately. [Insert paragraph about the claims you will*

discuss—use facts from the problem.] Let's analyze all of her legal claims based on the events of the last few weeks:

I. Assault
Lay out the legal test and standard.
Apply legal test to precise set of facts.
Conclusion about this claim.
[Write all of this in paragraph form. No bullet points.]

II. Battery
Same as before.

III. Intentional Infliction of Emotional Distress
Do it again.

IV. False Imprisonment
You're catching on!

V. Additional claims
Include analyses of those smaller issues that you think are relevant, and want to include to cover all your bases. Sometimes professors will throw in small issues just to see if you can identify and succinctly analyze them.

It looks like Tina has her hands full with this lawsuit! While she may be successful on her _____, _____, and _____ claims, it appears as if her _____ and _____ claims are a long-shot. [A few more sentences using your conclusions and drawing in the facts once again. Wrap it up and mention everything you concluded throughout the essay.]

As long as your essay is clearly organized, you reach a conclusion on your claims (always reach a conclusion as to who should win the legal argument—it shows that you are confident in your analysis and can argue for a client either way), and you know the correct legal standards, you'll do fine.

12

3.893475: Making the Grade and Rounding the Curve

Kelsey

> "The bottom line is that the grading process is horrible. In most classes, you get one chance at the end of the semester to prove yourself, and even that is dependent on ridiculous curves where only a certain percentage of students can get certain grades. Basically, there are no guarantees."
> —3L
>
> "I didn't realize that grades were the biggest deal. My classes are based on one test score a semester. Your entire worth is valued on what you do in 3 hours on one day."
> —2L

The above quotes might be a little misleading. Your law school grades aren't your *entire* worth—your mom will probably still love you if you fail. Apart from that, it's pretty spot-on.

The absolute most important thing you can know before starting law school is this: **your first semester grades are more important than any other.** Internships for the summer after 1L year will hire students based solely upon first semester grades, and large firms primarily judge you based on your first and second semester grades. So if there is ever a time to be concerned about grades, it's the first semester.

Once you've set your place in the class with your first semester grades, it is generally hard to jump around. After first semester grades come in, you will be ranked among the other people in your class; in three years, I've only moved two spots. I'm not a mathematician, so I can't give you statistics, but it seems to be the common experience that your average GPA and rank won't really ever change that dramatically. Somehow the first grades you get set the stage for your entire law school career. I'm not saying this to add more pressure, but it's something to know, and something no one ever told me.

Students commonly panic after receiving their first semester grades; if they do less than expected, they think their legal career is over. This isn't true. Grades are important, but they aren't so important as to dictate your legal career. Do your best, and you'll do fine. If you get your first semester grades back and are less than thrilled, take a middle-of-the-road approach: don't freak out, but don't ignore it, either. Schedule a meeting with each professor and go over your exams. Ask them for advice and try to understand your weaknesses. Learn from your mistakes and pay closer attention to your study habits. And maybe trade in some of your friends for smarter ones. (Kidding.)

If you didn't do as well as you would have liked, you're in good company. Most law schools employ a mandatory or suggested grading curve, at least for first year students. I'm not sure who devises the scales, but this rule ensures that only a certain number of students get As, A-s, B+s, all the way down. From a student's perspective, this can be both good and bad. This is good in the sense that **you never have to be the smartest person in the world; you just have to be the most strategic person in the room on a specified day**. The word strategic here is key. Law school is about strategy. GPAs are never a measurement of intelligence—how could they be? A class grade is based on how one professor perceives your exam, and taking an exam is primarily about strategy, not intelligence. If you can learn to successfully take an exam, you can learn to build a high GPA.

The grading curve is bad in that if you *aren't* the most strategic person in the room, the mathematical odds are stacked against you. The effect (or fairness) of the grading curve can be (and is) debated, but in the end, you can't do anything about it. If your law school employs a grading curve, chances are good that it won't immediately change protocol upon student protest. So you'll have to learn to suck it up. It's not that bad; no one *wants* you to do poorly. If anything, it's even *more* motivation to write a better exam than the guy next you. And that's what the whole grading thing is about.

OTHER Ls

13

You Want Me to Do *What?!*: Law Review[1]

Kelsey

"*I did it for my résumé.*"

—3L

"*Law review is the only worthwhile thing I've done in law school.*"

—3L

"*I don't know anything about it. Except that everyone I've talked to says they wish they hadn't done it.*"

—3L

The infamous law review. Almost every school has one, sometimes more, and, although I haven't been a member of multiple law reviews, I imagine they're all basically the same. So here's the deal: it really is as bad as everyone makes it out to be. It's a lot of work and it's a lot of stress. The work itself is tedious and time-consuming, unless you're on the Board or other highest committee, in which case the work is even *more* tedious and time-consuming. There are benefits, of course—huge benefits: it looks great on a résumé (invaluable in some cases), helps with writing skills, teaches you to cite correctly, etc., etc. But from the perspective of a law student with only semi-ambitious goals, the pros

---

1. A professor of mine once told me that the key to getting your law review article published is a good title, and the key to a good title is a colon (as in *Clever but Slightly Confusing Phrase: Clarification Sentence to Fully Explain Your Topic*).

might not outweigh the cons. If you do decide to join, go into it with your eyes open.

There are generally two different processes for obtaining membership starting your 2L fall, either used exclusively or in combination: the automatic, grade-determined candidacy process and the write-on candidacy process. If you are one of the lucky few who happen to land at the top of the class, you could be granted an automatic invitation to join law review. I suppose the theory is that you must be at the top of your class for a reason, and therefore must deserve membership. Good policy or not, the idea of automatic, grade-based candidacy is probably not going to disappear any time soon.

"Write-on" candidates (meaning all other students who want to join) enjoy a lengthier process, which requires writing an independent paper or drafting a legal memo to work out a pre-determined fictitious legal problem. These candidates may also have to meet certain grade requirements. The law review's level of prestige and selectiveness will dictate your chances of surviving the write-on process. People much smarter than I have written about the various strategies for success in this area, so I won't elaborate much further, except to say that the amount of work you put into your write-on assignment will be reflected in the journal's ultimate response to it.

At my law review, there was a candidacy period during which each potential member was expected to work for the law review without class credit while also drafting an independent legal paper of analytical significance. Our work for the law review during this period consisted almost exclusively of cite (footnote) checking— I spent hours checking the footnotes of articles that had already been written and selected for publication.

Learning correct citation use will be helpful when you start practicing and have to cite cases in briefs and memos. Your first year writing course or legal research class will attempt to teach you how to cite, but the only way to *really* learn is to do it over and over again, which is why the only people in law school who can correctly cite cases and other precedent quickly and easily have been on law review.

Your own paper will be subjected to the rigorous standards of your peers and will in all likelihood be very stressful to write, although it is a helpful exercise in critical thinking and thorough researching. Depending on the journal, it is entirely possible to be rejected as a member. Again, the prestige and selectiveness of the journal will dictate your chances of membership.

There are two reasons to join law review:

1. If you want to be a top student, with the best résumé possible, and the best[2] job prospects possible.

Granted, this is an immensely valid reason. Law review is an absolute necessity for a big firm job, a clerkship, or really any job with a competitive hiring process (which, these days, seems to be all of them). If you're *not* on law review and somehow manage to get an interview with a top firm, the first question they will ask you is, "why aren't you on law review?" and you better have a really good (even if fake) answer. You also better have a lot of other qualifications on your résumé to make up for the lack of law review membership. Participating on law review proves to an employer that you are capable of critical thinking and writing, and that you are willing to work hard. If you want to work at a big firm, or if you want to be a top student, do law review. Your résumé will thank you.

2. If you want to publish something.

If you know you have a knack for writing, or if you just want some sort of national (albeit *very* limited) attention, law review is a really great opportunity to be read. Usually law reviews will publish a few student articles a year, and if you play it right and write it well, you'll be thankful you put up with all the work. It's a big deal and a huge honor to be published as a student, and if you

---

2. By this I mean subjectively "best"—the jobs most people would consider the most prestigious: big firm jobs, judicial clerkships, research fellowships, etc. These jobs are the most prestigious, but just because they are the "best" might not make them the best for you. There's something to be said for florists with a law degree.

know you're a good writer, then by all means, give it a shot. Being published does wonders for a résumé, too, so this overlaps with reason #1 quite nicely. If you have any aims at a career in academia, or if you think you'd like to go on to an advanced degree program (LLM or SJD), publishing is what matters, and this is a wonderful first, and fairly accessible, opportunity. And, if nothing else, it's pretty cool that your article has the potential of being cited by any court or lawyer in the country.

I realize I am being slightly cynical in my analysis of legal journals here. Because, of course, there could be plenty of reasons to join law review. Maybe you're genuinely interested in legal writing and publishing. Maybe you like being a part of a team. Maybe you feel satisfaction from hard work. Maybe you have a crush on the person in charge. There could be any number of reasons to join law review and put in the work for two years. If you have your own reason for joining, that's great. But the majority of law students, in my experience, don't like to work hard just to work hard. Most people need a pretty good reason to put in that much time each semester devoted to, basically, an extracurricular activity.

To clarify my earlier assertion on this point, I will be more specific: from the perspective of an average, rational student, there are two main and widely-recognized reasons to join a legal journal. And my advice, which might seem somewhat contradictory to my earlier assertions but will turn out to be vital, would be that if you join law review, for these two reasons or any other, be prepared to work hard. Do not be one of those members who is in it just for the résumé-boost and who does subpar work, if any. There is a temptation to let the burden of the work fall on the shoulders of people who will pick up the slack. I, unfortunately, succumbed to this temptation on a number of occasions. But that's not fair. Just because you don't have altogether altruistic reasons for joining doesn't mean you can slide by once you get there; it's not fair to your classmates or to the journal. Think hard before the time comes to join law review and if you opt in, fulfill all your obligations to the best of your ability.

I joined law review mainly because I thought I should. I was invited to "grade" on to my school's legal journals. If I hadn't been,

13 • YOU WANT ME TO DO *WHAT?!*: LAW REVIEW

I'm not sure I would have had the interest to "write" on. Being too preoccupied with arranging my 1L study abroad trip, I didn't do any research into the responsibilities of law review or the differences between the journals at my school. The day of the deadline to make a commitment, which fell in the middle of my 1L summer, which *also* happened to be in the middle of my trip to Ireland, I spontaneously committed myself to my school's largest journal.

My selection of journals came down to a minor comment that I remembered a professor making once. He noted that this particular journal was, in his opinion, *the* one to join. So I did. Another appealing aspect of this journal was that no one tried to recruit me. During my study abroad program, I had an experience with a member of another journal where I felt pressured to accept its invitation to join; this kind of recruitment style had the opposite effect on me, and I was relieved to remain somewhat anonymous as a candidate for the other, larger journal.

I joined law review with the same mindset I approached law school with, and the same mindset with which I approach almost everything in my life: if I don't like it, I'll just quit. I assured myself that this wasn't like the Army, and there was really no harm in trying it out. Like I said, at this point, I really had no idea what law review would entail.

Journal orientation, held at the end of the summer before 2L year, was overwhelming to say the least. After only a year of law school, I had no idea how to correctly cite cases and periodicals using *Bluebook* rules, or how to find original sources for obscure references. I was also overwhelmed by the tediousness of the tasks assigned, which can't be avoided but certainly can't be celebrated either. In fact, as a testament to the journal's overwhelming atmosphere, my assigned partner dropped out after only two hours of orientation. If I hadn't been so nervous, I probably would have followed him.

By far the most overwhelming aspect of joining law review was the concept of writing a paper on an original legal topic full of interesting and noteworthy analysis, commonly referred to as a "note" or "comment." ("Notes" generally refer to pieces analyzing a specific case, while "comments" generally refer to pieces on a specific topic, using as references many cases and other sources.) The hardest part of this assignment, at least for me, was figuring out where to start. If you're interested in certain areas of the law already, choosing a topic won't be quite as challenging for you. If you have no idea what you're interested in, choosing a topic will prove to be arduous. I fell into the latter category: I hadn't yet decided what part of the law appealed to me, which might still be true to some extent. This is the sort of problem that emerges when one has too many options. With an entire world of legal issues available to me, I had absolutely no clue which tiny piece I should write about.

A day before my final topic was due to the law review paper committee, I happened to see an interesting news story on a morning talk show which involved a woman suing her ex-fiancé. This became the basis for my law review comment. Seeing that news story was a great jumping-off point and allowed me to research and narrow down an area of the law that was fascinating, if not readily taught in first-year classes. After being on the writing end of a comment and, later, the reviewing end of candidate comments, I understand the importance of topic selection for a law review article. For a paper to have a good chance of being published, it must be unique, narrow, and quirky, and also contain original, compelling arguments. In addition, it must be well written and thoroughly researched.

The semester I spent writing my comment was stressful, to put it kindly. I pulled several all-nighters, sacrificed a room in my house to books, copies of journal articles, binders, and treatises, and annoyed everyone I knew with "interesting" tidbits about my topic. In the end, I had a 45-page paper (with over 400 footnotes) to show for it, and was thrilled with the result. Preparing a paper of this significance for the first time was a major achievement, and I was proud of the effort I had put into it.

Once the candidacy period ended and I was a full-fledged member of law review, my duties mainly consisted of subciting (or cite-checking), which essentially means reviewing the footnotes in scholarly articles for accuracy. There are other functions to be found within a journal, however. Depending on your law review's structure, there could be purely administrative or financial positions, which will be more appealing if you're not into research or editing. Check into the positions available and the steps necessary to get them (including the election process).

Becoming a member means subjecting yourself to elections and other voting issues of the journal, which are inherently always student-run. Like any other organization, these processes tend to feel very political and somewhat fake, almost like sorority or fraternity "rushing." You will parade yourself and your achievements in front of your peers in order to gain a position of power within the journal which, to be fair, is probably the only way to elect officers within a student organization. I tried to remove myself from this as much as possible; creating or fostering drama within a law review is exhausting and turns out to be a waste of time. The best rule of thumb for getting elected to a position is to be normal, work hard, and follow protocol, without being arrogant or deceptive.

I can't say that I loved the type of work law review required or the camaraderie of my classmates. I also can't say that I worked as hard as I should have. But I *can* say that I do not regret being a member of law review, and I proffer that it is one of the main reasons I was afforded certain opportunities, including major job opportunities. Law review got me a job and facilitated my first published article and for that I am thankful. Law review was a wonderful venue in which to practice my writing, which has become increasingly important.

Even though I do not regret my decision to become a member of a legal journal, there were times, occasionally in the middle of the night, when I would find myself doing journal work and wishing I were hanging out with my friends instead. Both of my co-authors opted not to join law review, and I think they would both tell you that they don't regret their decisions either. Like almost everything else in law school, it's a balancing test and a personal decision, to be made only after researching and weighing your options.

14

Mock Trial and Error

Samantha

> "I've gained so much from my trial competition experience: organizational skills, speaking skills, and the opportunity to network with attorneys and professors who judge the competitions."
>
> —3L
>
> "I think it's a good thing to have on your résumé, but I'm not sure competing is enough to make an employer take notice. You'll probably need to place in a national competition for it to really matter."
>
> —3L

Trial competitions are called many different things, including variations of "mock trial," "moot court," or "advocacy practice." I'll refer to them all simply as "mock trial" for the sake of brevity. Keep in mind that each individual trial organization has its strengths and weaknesses and will vary by school. Your law school may offer several options under the trial competition umbrella, or just one. But, they all basically serve the same purpose: to give students a chance to have a near-real life experience in the courtroom. Though nothing can entirely prepare you for the moment you step into the courtroom as a practicing attorney, this is the experience that (supposedly) comes closest.

In a mock trial, you will act as the attorney for a specified mock client. You will attempt to resolve "real" legal problems in "real" litigation. Trial competitions sometimes focus solely on one area of the law, say environmental law or criminal law, or are broad enough to include all appellate-style actions. Generally, these competitions will be held at your school and will be hosted by one of your school's mock trial organizations. You might have to be a member of that particular organization to compete, which can usually be accomplished with a brief application and a membership fee. Some competitions are for solo attorneys, meaning you compete alone, while others allow a team of attorneys.

If you are on your school's mock trial team, you might compete in regional or national competitions. Depending on the level of involvement at your school, it may be tough to secure a spot on the competing team because these competitions are ... competitive, for lack of a better term. The experiences I've heard from my school's traveling trial team sound ridiculous. These students prepare for an entire semester, sometimes more, for a few hours of actual advocacy in front of a select panel of judges. Once the competition has ended, or the team is out of the running, the students are free to enjoy a paid stay in a nice city. This is where some of the ridiculousness comes in, because a semester's worth of preparation has been exhausted in a single day, and people will feel the need to decompress. Which is fine. Just make sure no one has a camera at the mock trial after-party.

Needless to say, mock trial is not for everyone. But if you think you want to be a trial lawyer, give it a shot. Extra experience never hurt anyone. If you don't like it, that's probably a pretty good indicator that you may not like being a trial attorney. Then again, you might love it, and be good at it. There's only one way to find out.

One student who is involved with mock trial told me that it's only worth it for those students who want to be trial lawyers. "Worth it" in the résumé-boosting, job-seeking sense. Mock trial requires a substantial time commitment and if you're not sure you want to be involved, then you should look into what the program entails before signing up. On the other hand, if you think you want to be a trial lawyer or litigator, then mock trial experience is crucial. You will perfect the skills needed to be a good trial lawyer, and it always helps to have a head start. But perhaps just as important, you'll become comfortable in the courtroom spotlight. The most important skill for a trial lawyer (so I've heard) is the

14 • MOCK TRIAL AND ERROR

ability to speak comfortably, clearly, and concisely in front of people. It's a good idea to work on this skill in law school, before you have clients depending on your performance.

In addition to mock trial teams and competitions you sign up for, you may be required to do mock trials in some of your classes. Even if a course like this is not required, think about taking it anyway, regardless of whether or not you want to be a trial lawyer. The setting is far less formal and adversarial than any official mock trial competition, but it nevertheless helps in mastering skills essential to lawyering, including critical thinking, advocating on someone's behalf, and thinking on your feet. It's also kind of fun, or at least a nice break from the usual structure of a lecture class.

You won't necessarily be judged for your performance as a fake lawyer in this situation—though you should expect criticism, commentary, and clarification from your professor. Oh, and a grade. And you won't win anything if you do really well, except pride and bragging rights. Of course, your classmates will probably judge you on your performance, but only if it is particularly terrible or unnecessarily dramatic. In the event that you *are* unnecessarily dramatic, expect the entire school to know within minutes. In my experience with a class that required us to hold fake trials, one student fled the courtroom in tears when the witness (*fake* witness, may I remind you) wasn't cooperating (in the *fake* case). That sort of performance will earn you a reputation, though probably not a good one.

Whether in class or not, participation in mock trial competitions and less formal trials allows a law student to gain confidence in those skills necessary to becoming a trial lawyer while being subjected to pressures unique to the courtroom. As an added benefit, you will meet new people and network with other future attorneys. There's no real downside to trying it out; you can always decide that you would rather pursue other extracurricular activities. But in the best scenario, you'll gain some experience and learn a thing or two ... which is what law school is for, anyway.

15

I See London, I See France

Elizabeth

> "*Studying abroad for a summer is awesome. Do it.*"
>
> —3L

> "*I loved studying abroad, but it didn't help me find a job, or even pick a career path. I wish I had found an internship abroad instead of wasting summer months on a glorified vacation.*"
>
> —3L

Unlike many law students, I went overseas twice during my L years. While I had already developed a great appreciation for study abroad programs before law school, I don't think every law student realizes how valuable they are.

It may seem counter-intuitive that a study abroad program, which is by definition in another country, will further your legal education when you are interested in learning U.S. law (and practicing in the U.S.). Hopefully I'm not the first to break the news, but we are now living in an extremely interconnected and international world. Regardless of whether you want to be a local criminal attorney or an international business transactions attorney, you will most likely be faced with some version of international law, or an international problem, during your career. Exposing yourself to other legal systems will at least give you a rudimentary appreciation for international legal issues, and real life is a more effective teacher than a textbook; sitting in a foreign courtroom will be more beneficial than taking an "International Law" class at your school in the U.S. As an added bonus, you might have the chance to learn about different or peculiar areas of law that your school doesn't offer courses in.

An invaluable component of studying abroad is the inherently non-U.S. locale. You will most likely be outside of your comfort zone, which seems to be a recurring theme in our "expand-your-knowledge-and-make-yourself-smarter" lessons. The language may be different, the food a bit weird, and the culture unlike anything you have experienced before. As a student, this is the easiest time to learn flexibility and to adapt quickly to new situations. Studying abroad will almost definitely foster this. If you have never traveled outside the U.S., this is your chance—all with the blessing of your dean.

If used strategically, studying abroad can also serve as a résumé-building and networking tool. Study abroad programs bring people together from various law schools around the U.S. and within the host country. With 20–40 students in a program, you are making that many more connections and friendships, as well as opening your own eyes to the rest of the world. Having connections in Australia and the Netherlands will go a long way to broadening your job search if you're interested in international positions. If you're interested in practicing in the town where you grew up, international letters of recommendation will be monumentally impressive.

There is something you should realize when browsing different study abroad programs. Many law schools offer study abroad programs that are nothing more than international vacations for class credit. Don't get me wrong—these are really, really fun. Grown men and women will revert to their younger, wilder ways and depending on where you choose to go, your study abroad experience may resemble more of a frat party than an intellectual summit. Again, I'm not knocking these. If you've never been to a foreign country, this will be a blast and, of course, it is what you make it; you are responsible for your experience, and if you want a serious, cultural exchange, it's entirely possible. Samantha and Kelsey both tell stories to this day of unbelievable experiences with classmates on their respective study abroad programs. Somehow, law students think they have a free pass, behavior-wise, when they're studying abroad. This is not the case. What happens abroad *does not* stay abroad. Your rendezvous with the police in a tiny Italian town will be the "talk" of the Internet social world, and your unfortunate incident in a Chinese karaoke bar will be frozen in time in 600 photos. You will hear this warning throughout every chapter of this book: **do not be an idiot.** If you enroll in a study abroad program just for the experience of being abroad, that's fine, but be smart. Or at least discreet.

Aside from the potential of foreign horseplay, the biggest downside to these relaxed, vacation-like study abroad programs is the lack of work experience available to add to your résumé. While everyone else is home with their nose to the grindstone learning the ropes of working in a law firm, you will be sipping espresso in an Argentine café. Granted, the café is probably a lot more enjoyable, but it's not the huge career booster you might think. In fact, an employer will look at a generic study abroad experience as nothing more than a topic of conversation during your interview. If you even get that far. But don't despair—there are two viable options to ensure you get the best of both worlds during your summer.

First, you could try to schedule your summer so that you can work (at a firm, as a volunteer at a legal clinic, or doing research for a professor) for half the summer and go abroad for the other half. With a lot of big firms offering half-summer positions, this might work during your 2L summer as well as your 1L summer. The best strategy is to study abroad your 1L summer, however, since paid positions are much harder to come by with only one year of school under your belt. 2L summer is the optimum time for work experience, but if you're adventurous enough, it could also accommodate an experience abroad.

Many schools offer different study abroad programs with start dates throughout the year, so careful research will provide you with multiple options. Be savvy, fire up Google (or Bing—again, we're not discriminatory), and find the program that will be the best fit for you. A study abroad program (or glorified vacation) combined with relevant legal work will ensure that you don't have a gaping hole on the "Experience" portion of your résumé.

The second option can be a little more difficult to orchestrate. When you line up a study abroad program, ask the director whether there are internship opportunities available in that country, either through the program or independently. Most program directors try to help you find something; remember, they know a lot more people than you do. If the program itself offers internship opportunities, **take advantage of them**. It might be hard to pass up a month-long program where you have class only once a week and act like obnoxious foreigners the other six days (you will be *those* Americans), but it will ultimately be worth it. The study abroad program Kelsey attended offered several 6-week internships in the host country, without the hassle of job-hunting. The sole reason she didn't sign up for one was because she was more interested in *being* abroad than *studying* abroad. Looking back, I think she would tell you that she missed a wonderful opportunity to gain work experience and expand her list of references. Drinking Irish coffees for two months was probably also much less enlightening than an internship with a foreign governmental agency.

Work experience abroad gives you the same benefit as work experience in the U.S. but with one major advantage, at least to an adventurous type: you'll be in another country. Contact the director of the study abroad program as soon as you sign up about possible internship opportunities, and look into well-established organizations in the host country that may have outside opportunities. If you are choosing a study abroad opportunity that isn't offered through your university, do not expect a lot of internal support in terms of funding your internship. After all, this is not your school's program, and they mostly likely will not know a lot about it. Expect to spend a significant amount of time researching the area, the program, and the available opportunities. You may end up sending out a lot of blind inquiries but in the end, all you need is one positive response. It's not always an easy process to locate an international internship, but it is possible, and it is worth it.

When I was accepted to a study abroad program in South Africa sponsored by a university in another state, which I had found myself through hours of online research, I began looking for a way to extend my time there to include an internship experience. Since the program itself only lasted for half the summer, I was hoping to find an opportunity to work for six weeks after my classes ended. The program was offered through another university, which meant my law school wasn't able to help me procure an internship in South Africa, as the school didn't have a network set up in that country. It was also hard to get help from the sponsoring university because it was states away, and I had never met any of the directors in person. Nevertheless, I was able to research local agencies and, with the assistance of my sponsoring university, I applied for volunteer internships in South Africa. And, in the end, I found the perfect, half-summer opportunity. But the trick was, *I* had to find it; it wasn't going to find me. And then I had to find a place to stay, and arrange for my own visa ... you know the rest.

But don't let any of this scare you. Each of this book's authors participated in a study abroad program. I studied abroad my 1L summer in Argentina through my law school and worked and studied in South Africa my 2L summer. Samantha went to China her 1L summer through her law school—and managed to coordinate her study abroad experience with the Summer Olympics (an impressive feat). Kelsey studied abroad in Ireland her 1L summer through her law school and spent half of her 2L summer in a major U.S. city going to art school—because she had always wanted to. We each gave up valuable summer months to go out and experience the world—and we each survived. We are no less marketable or hireable because of our summer choices, and we are more interesting people for them.

Academically speaking, studying abroad is not necessarily the best method of boosting your résumé, ensuring you have a job after graduation, or even raising your GPA. But it will help you to become a more well-rounded and interesting person, not to mention give you an expanded network of individuals in your chosen field. It will at least give you a Facebook profile picture that will make your friends—or grandma—jealous.

16

Why Researching in Your Underwear Might Be a Bad Idea

Kelsey

I do not expect you to take my advice on this one. I do not take my own advice on this a lot of the time. This is something you will learn for yourself because you will not believe me now. I just hope you learn this lesson sooner rather than later. Here it is: legal research using actual, physical books (to be found in the antiquated building that is the library) is much easier than online legal research.

This is an extraordinary concept to many of us. How can a pile of dusty books be more convenient than our answer to everything else: the Internet? That's why you won't understand ... until one day you do. You will take a legal research class your first year, and you will get the run-down on how to find cases, statutes, and almost everything else. You will also be given access to online legal research sites. Many schools will give you a password to these sites immediately; some schools will force you to use the books for a certain period of time before granting you access to these (do not be angry if you go to one of these schools—be grateful).

Online methods are instrumental in legal research because they allow you to get the most updated, thorough information available. You can easily check the status of cases and laws, as well as any references or related information. Another very handy feature of online research is the ability to retrieve a case or statute at the click of a button. If you know exactly what you want, there is no quicker way to retrieve it than online. And, you can write a brief in your PJs (or underwear)—that's huge. The benefits of online legal research are clear, abundant, and important. My advice is not meant to knock online research. To the contrary, I want to reinforce the idea that *despite* the advantages of online research, you still need to learn and appreciate the old-fashioned version of the Internet: the library.

Legal research books, which you will learn *all* about in your legal research class, were designed to help you narrow down your focus and find an answer to a specific question. These books have been around for decades and, believe it or not, have created an efficient system of research. The problem with online research is the breadth of information. When you have a legal problem to solve and don't know where to begin, the research websites will be overwhelming. It's extremely hard to narrow the millions of documents available when you don't know exactly what you're looking for. Word searches will be difficult to tailor to your specific legal question, and the results even harder to filter. In short, the problem with using online research methods exclusively is that there is too *much* information available at your fingertips, and filtering through it all will waste more time than is necessary. There are, of course, ways of reducing this problem, and you could probably teach yourself to be the most efficient online researcher in all the land. Assuming you are a normal student, however, you will probably not be classically trained in Boolean searches.

Another practical advantage of learning to research with books while in school is the online-research-as-crack analogy. Law students are given unlimited access to online research websites (Westlaw and LexisNexis) while in school. For free. In real life, these websites are monstrously expensive, and many smaller employers cannot afford to use them or can only afford to use them in moderation. So the analogy is that you, as a student, will become addicted to this vast, exciting, and free world of online research, and when you become an actual lawyer, it will be quickly taken away from you. That's when the withdrawals start, and you will have no idea what to do. Seeing as there is no Westlaw Withdrawal Support Group around (to the best of my knowledge), you'd be much better off knowing how to survive without it while you're in school.

During law school, you will take a legal research class. You will write a few short memos or briefs and probably prepare a research

16 · RESEARCHING IN YOUR UNDERWEAR

paper. But you will not *actually* research. At least not in a meaningful sense. This is inevitable, because law school can only present you with hypothetical problems to research, instead of actual, urgent legal needs. You will not experience the urgency of real legal research until you are presented with an urgent legal problem.

When I briefly worked with a local law firm, I was instructed to keep my online legal research to a minimum, even though I had access to the company code. Terrified as I was of making a mistake, I went the better-safe-than-sorry road and forbade myself to even log on, for fear that I would lose track of time and rack up the hourly fees. I didn't have any experience with library research outside my first semester legal research class; I researched everything online when writing my law review article and in every previous job (which I later came to regret). So, naturally, I panicked. I was forced to re-teach myself how to research with a book. Although the natural high of fear kicked in to speed up my memory, it would have been a much less intimidating task had I been more comfortable with all the various methods of research. At the end of my time at the firm, I understood just how efficient that musty old library can be.

Again, you will never let go of online research entirely, nor would anyone want you to. For many aspects of research, a book will not help you. But for an increasingly online world, you need to know that library research is still an integral tool in learning how to effectively solve legal problems. Learn and appreciate both methods while you're in school, because it is much better to experiment with different ways of learning as a student than as an attorney—no one can sue you for student malpractice.

17

Wait … That Class Is at 8 a.m.? On Fridays? L No!

Samantha

> "I've been surprised by how the classes I've taken have actually been interesting. When I saw my first semester schedule, and saw that I would be taking just Torts and Contracts, I thought there was no hope."
>
> —2L

Organizing your schedule and selecting your classes: *what* a dilemma! Okay, not really even an issue until your second year, and even then, it's not really much of a dilemma, but worth some thought nonetheless. The first year is easy enough; your 1L schedule will essentially be predetermined for you. Expect to take the standard 1L lecture classes like Contracts, Torts, Civil Procedure, and Constitutional Law. You'll also probably take a legal writing class and a legal research class. After your first year, though, academic freedom ensues, aside from the few additional required courses you will need to take as a 2L or 3L. Of course, "academic freedom" is a relative term and only means that you can choose from any law school course offered in any given semester. It boils down to this: you get to choose your classes based on your interests.

You might discover that this newly acquired freedom to determine your own fate suddenly evokes a fear of the same. While there's certainly a continuum of options and routes that students take, here are two basic routes to consider: take as many bar courses as you can or take courses because they sound interesting.

I guess this is the part where I explain what a "bar course" is and why it matters. A bar course is any course that covers an area of the law that will be tested on the bar exam. A simple example of a bar course is one of your first year lecture courses; they are the important classes—fundamental to passing the bar. These topics will most likely be tested on every state's bar exam. To many students' dismay, your final exam in Contracts will not be the last time you have to deal with contract issues.

Consider your ultimate goals when deciding which classes to take. Are you looking to build a solid foundation of bar topics prior to bar review? Are you still exploring different areas of the law? Do you have a specific area of interest already? Are you generally apathetic?

The two most common, though not mutually exclusive, approaches to class selection are:

> **The unadulterated bar course approach.** All bar courses, all the time. Some students try to take as many bar courses as possible over the course of their three years of law school in preparation for the bar exam. This is not a wholly inadvisable approach. In fact, it makes a lot of practical sense. After all, these are the subjects you will be tested on during the bar exam, so you could get a head start on mastering them now. This approach arguably makes for a stereotypically well-rounded legal education, i.e., what the exemplary lawyer *should* know. A good approach for some—a not-so-good approach for others. While it does make practical sense, some students have interests that expand far beyond the boundaries of the bar exam, and want to expand their learning potential, as well. You certainly don't want to find yourself resenting law school altogether because you don't like any of your classes.
>
> **The these-courses-sound-interesting approach.** If you fear you might resent a course about secured transactions or wills and estates, stick to this approach. And, maybe there will be some overlap between courses that sound interesting to you and bar courses, which is always a pleasant sur-

17 • THAT CLASS IS AT 8 A.M.? ON FRIDAYS? L NO!

prise.[1] You will cover bar topics in your review course prior to taking the bar exam. So, unless a bar course is required by your school, don't think you *need* to take bar courses in order to have a chance at passing the bar. Sure, it can't hurt—but it might not be worth it to spend your valuable academic hours taking classes you have no interest in. This approach may result in you taking zero bar courses after your first-year requirements. If you are comfortable with this approach, embrace it. Take the classes you want to take solely because you want to take them.

A variation of this method is to focus on classes that will help you establish your commitment to a certain area of law or a certain type of job. This means taking course like Administrative Law or Legislation if you're interested in government work, or a class like Criminal Adjudication if you're interested in criminal defense. Although perhaps a little less enjoyable than a full-blown class selection free-for-all, it should line up fairly well with the classes that interest you. A select grouping of courses will lend support to your claims when you market yourself to an employer. It will also give you a head start on learning about certain fields in which you may ultimately practice.

I took this approach. I selected my classes based on what was appealing to me. I enrolled in a class about the death penalty because it sounded interesting, and I liked the professor. I took classes I wanted to take, without any other real motivation.

The value of a good professor cannot be overstated. Another good way to approach class selection is to focus on who teaches a class. Good professors can make any class interesting and enjoyable, not to mention beneficial. You will quickly realize which pro-

---

1. I once heard this conversation between two third-year students:
Student 1: "I didn't take *any* bar courses!"
Student 2: "Yes, you did. Family Law, Civil Procedure, Criminal Procedure ..."
Student 1: "Oh. Well, I didn't *mean* to. They just sounded good."
Students 1 and 2 may happen to be my co-authors. But I'm not pointing fingers.

fessors you relate to best and which professors just don't do it for you. This will not always coincide with their reputations, which is fine. You know your learning style, and you know what's best for you; trust your instincts.

A very extreme example of the professor-oriented approach is taking a class in which you have *no* interest just because you like the professor. During her 2L year, Kelsey elected to take a Sports Law class. And one defining feature of her personality *certainly* cannot be overstated: Kelsey *hates* sports. While everyone in the (all-male) class was debating the politics of the BCS, she politely smiled and doodled on her notepad until the conversation came back around to the relevant aspects of the law. But the class was enjoyable to her for several reasons: she had a great professor, she met people in her class that she didn't already know, and she was able to experience an aspect of the law that had been completely foreign to her just months before. Even though the class didn't initially sound interesting, it was. Stepping outside your comfort zone with a professor you're comfortable with is never a bad idea.

An additional consideration to class selection is whether your school offers programs whereby you can "specialize" in a particular area of the law. For example, if you are interested in international law and your school offers a program in international law, you might want to take the required courses in order to get that certificate. Or you may realize in your 3L year that you've just *accidentally* taken four courses that help satisfy the requirements of the international law certificate. If this happens, it might be worth it to go ahead and meet the other requirements. Either way, you'll have a "specialty" on your résumé, whether it was intended or not, and that will help distinguish you from your peers when it comes time to find a job.

Choosing your classes isn't such a big deal; it comes down to personal preference in the end. There are, of course, certain considerations to keep in mind, but any path you choose will lead you to the same place: graduation. I won't even tell you not to choose classes based on when they are offered. There's something to be said for only having class two days a week your last semester, and those 8 a.m. classes can be brutal. Heck, you'll probably even graduate if you use a dart-board-selection approach to classes. Just make sure to enjoy yourself and have as much fun as you can with your legal education.

18

Find a Stranger

Kelsey

> "Whenever a relationship ends, one party will always think it ended badly. Then everyone at school hates you."
> —3L
>
> "It's easy for rumors to spread, and it's even easier to alienate people."
> —2L
>
> "There are no normal people in law school. Except for me. And I can't date myself."
> —3L

This section could have alternatively been titled: *There Is Life Outside Your Law School*; *What Happens in Law School Doesn't Stay in Law School*; *Law School Relationships: The Good, the Bad, and the Absolutely Outrageous*, and so on and so forth. But I'm sticking with *Find a Stranger*, so we'll go from there.

Law schools have a tendency to create a very insular environment. Law schools also have a tendency to feel *just* like high school. There are hallways filled with rows upon rows of lockers and posters advertising talent shows, proms, and elections taped to every wall ... how much more *Saved by the Bell* does it get? Much like high school, you will get to know everyone in your classes and will be subjected to numerous pieces of gossip on a daily basis about who's sleeping with whom, who's smarter than whom, and who punched whom in the parking lot. While I cannot officially sanction this conduct, I cannot wholly condemn it either. There is a lot to be said for law school gossip. Until you're the topic du jour.

You will (hopefully) make a lot of (great) friends in law school. Something about the stress and fear of the whole thing creates a really unique bond; making new friends will come easily because you never lack for conversation, starting with how scary a professor is or where on earth you're supposed to find a statute book. The plethora of law-school-students-only activities and social events will only serve to enhance these friendships. These are all good things. But remember: **there is life outside of law school.** There are other interesting topics to debate and other interesting people to meet.[1] Make an effort to keep in touch with college friends, high school friends, and work friends, because you will need to take a break from law school. Having outside friends and interests will put everything in perspective and help to break up the tiny little world that law school creates.

Law students sometimes talk about not having enough time to do anything; this is misleading. There is always time for family, friends, and the truly important pieces of your life that have nothing to do with school. Do not become so wrapped up in your new world that you lose your old self. This isn't to say that you shouldn't get involved, and make friends in school: you absolutely should. But realize that law school should become a part of your life, and not the other way around.

Taking time away from law school includes taking time for yourself. Go to the gym, take walks with your family, shower daily. Samantha managed to run several marathons during her tenure in law school without sacrificing her GPA or her sanity. And I also was able to run over six miles (non-consecutively) during my three years(!). All three of us even became law school co-ed softball champions in the intramural league.[2]

Not to overemphasize the point or encourage bad study habits, but you should enjoy your time in law school as much as possible.

---

[1]. If this means coercing a "barfriender" (bartender + friend) into listening to you complain about everything there is to complain about, then so be it. Just be sure to tip well.

[2]. There is no proof of this. In fact, although I don't *exactly* remember the *exact* outcomes of each season, I remember *feeling* like a winner.

During our 3L year, for example, we took three major road trips together (ranging from Durango to Austin to Dollywood), and individually we traveled to Vegas, North Carolina, Denver, Portland, and San Antonio. We took classes at the gym, had standing coffee dates with friends, and went to movies on weeknights. We had fun, and made the most of being in school.

Even with these major, and non-major, activities to keep us sane, we probably still lost ourselves in some bad decisions, a seemingly inevitable result of the law school world. Law students tend to pick up bad habits: drinking, smoking, and eating poorly. Now, this approach can be appealing. It creates an outward manifestation of the stress involved with your graduate education. It's a way of showing the world that you're tired and working really, really hard. So yes, I can see how this approach is appealing. And sometimes, it's even more subconscious than that.

The outside, non-lawyer world talks about how the law is a drinking profession and will make jokes about attorneys with alcohol problems. I haven't yet determined whether people in law school drink to live up to their stereotypes or whether attorneys drink to relive their days in law school. Either way, it's a pretty stable part of the law school environment; there is a *lot* of drinking. I know we're all adults here, so I won't tell you what to do. It's fine to have fun. Just be careful. And I speak from experience on this one.

It's important not to let yourself go just because you're a law student. It's not worth it. Being a student shouldn't allow you to feel as if you have an excuse for bad behavior. Other students aren't the only people who will be talking about you. We spoke to one professor who said his biggest problem with law students was that, all too often, they developed bad personal habits while in law school. Even during the course of our brief interview, at least fifteen students perched themselves outside his office window, taking a smoke break on the patio. He motioned to the crowd, which was shivering in the snow just to catch some nicotine relief, and noted that it's entirely unnecessary to lose all discipline due to stress. We agree. Don't develop bad habits because it's easy or expected. And if you had these habits before law school, break them.

I won't give you my stop-smoking lecture (okay, I will: stop smoking), but I will say this: **people hate the smelly kid in class.** If you're a smoker, you smell. I don't care how much spray you use, or how far away from the building you stand. You smell. And no one will want to sit next to you. There is nothing worse than coming back from a class break and being acutely aware that you're suddenly unable to breathe due to the overwhelming smoke trailing the students who just *had* to run out and take a smoke break. I have actually switched seats in a class, and talked to the professor in order to alter the seating chart, just so I could avoid the smoker. People hate the smelly kid in class, and the last thing you want is for people to hate you. After all, you're stuck with these people for three years.

There are a lot of different aspects to the relationships you form while in law school. You will likely meet the most wonderful and most awful people you will ever know. They will be both fascinating and dull, sweet and slimy; it really does run the gamut. But be aware going into it that no matter how much you get along with someone, or *don't* as the situation might be, these fellow students will eventually become your professional colleagues.

I won't tell you to be nice to people, because at this juncture in your life, I'm assuming you've either established a decent personality or have become a jackass, and if you're a jackass, you probably don't want advice on how to correct that unfortunate flaw. So let's assume you're a decently nice individual. Good for you. Unfortunately, this might not be enough.

You know that extremely drunken rant you laid on your classmate at the Halloween party for getting a better grade than you? That's what he'll be picturing when you call him up asking for a job in ten years. And that super skanky dance you displayed at Law Prom?[3] That's what the judge, your current classmate, will be envisioning when you argue your case in front of her in twenty. Your behavior has repercussions that last well beyond the next morn-

---

3. It would be much more exciting if you were in optometry school, because then you would get to go to the Eye Ball. But, alas, we're stuck with Barrister's Ball, or, for us commoners, Law Prom.

ing's hangover; from hallway gossip to a law firm rejection letter, people will remember you, for better or worse. Be (at least somewhat) smart, and realize that you are setting a precedent for yourself with your behavior that won't only affect you for three years, but will follow you throughout your career.

In a somewhat different type of relationship, dating in law school can pose its own problems. While much can be said about law school dating, the brunt of it pretty much boils down to the nature of a law school environment: limited, self-contained, and gossipy. There will be couples in your class or section. Some will succeed, and some will fail.

Some students will avoid the situation altogether by being married or otherwise taken during law school, while others will only create *more* drama by being married or otherwise taken (as inter-Section infidelity gossip seems to spread faster than most other kinds). Imagine this modern fairy tale: a student marries his college sweetheart 1L year, takes this pretty new wife to a school-sponsored, alcohol-soaked party 2L year, watches said wife "meet" his fellow students on the dance floor, and divorces adulterous princess 3L year. Sounds far-fetched, I know, but stranger things have happened.

In three years, we've seen plenty of absolutely absurd law school relationships, ranging from the awkward public makeout sessions to the serial online relationshipper. I will say this: if you find yourself in one officially-sanctioned (i.e., Facebook-recognized) law school relationship after another, with men who all appear to be *friends* with each other (and somehow don't mind passing off a girlfriend), people will talk about you. We know, because we did.

No one can tell you whether or not to enter the law school dating pool, but realize that your personal business will undoubtedly become fodder for all the people who know your name but who have never, and will never, know you. And if your law school relationship (or "relationship" as the case may be) does sour, as some inevitably do, understand that the awkward "I bumped into my ex" experiences will be multiplied in awkwardness and will occur *every day*. Social circles will split, and friends will take sides. I know we're all (supposedly) adults, but these things tend to happen, often without fault but with plenty of blame. And yes, sometimes, maybe often, law school dating relationships succeed. But if you're going to play the game, be aware of the potential consequences of one bad decision.

Which brings me to my last point: **if you're single, and especially if you're not, don't make out with someone from law school that you'd be ashamed to tell your best friend about.** Because not only will your best friend find out, so will the other 250 people in your class. And they will make fun of you. A lot.

19

E-mails, Volunteering, and How to Get a Job: Oh My!

Elizabeth

Law school keeps you busy. Between classes, reading, and other extracurricular activities, your time will be booked and, after *these* obligations are met, you will still have family and non-law school responsibilities weighing you down. From this, you will learn a powerful lesson in time management. Before these seemingly competing obligations arose, I wish I would have known how important campus meetings could be.

When you start school, or even before, you will be given a school e-mail address. Novel? Not quite. With this address you will be gifted with/bombarded with e-mails about joining organizations, supporting the angel tree at Christmas, attending upcoming guest speakers, and much, much more. After a while, the excitement of law school will wear off, and these e-mails will start to get annoying. You will stop reading them and send them directly to the tiny little e-mail trash bin without passing Go and collecting two hundred dollars.[1] Don't do this. This is worth repeating: **don't ignore campus and school announcements**, even if in e-mail form.

As time consuming as it may be, at least *skim* the e-mails you get (this means open and read a few words)—at the *very* least if they come from a faculty or staff member. That way, if an obscure e-mail about a lunch meeting comes in, you will know two things: a) you will get a free lunch and b) you will learn about a potential

---

1. Much like recruiters and other potential employers will do to your e-mail attachment of a résumé.

career opportunity, networking opportunity, or bar exam guidance. Law schools often conduct very helpful meetings covering almost anything you have questions about; however, law schools also tend to fail miserably at advertising these meetings in an effective way. You may see an e-mail advising you of an upcoming meeting about "Clerkships," but since you have no idea what a clerkship is, you will have no reason to care and even less reason to attend. Three years later you will complain that you wish you had known what a clerkship was so that you could have applied for one.

Perhaps part of the problem is that a law school administration assumes you will care about everything they offer; therefore, they need not fully explain or advertise their meetings beforehand, because they expect you to attend regardless. As students, we sympathize with you that this is unreasonable. Most students have pretty narrow blinders on. If it "doesn't apply" to us, we won't go. And, there is a tendency to think that things we don't understand "don't apply" to us as students. Short of a law school administration crash course in how to force-feed students information (outside of the force-feeding that is an actual law school class), the obligation falls on you to seek out and absorb as much as you can about as much as you can. That's why the advice "read your e-mails and go to meetings," which may seem simple at best and silly at worst, is probably the best way to get you the information you will ultimately want. If you start this practice early in your law school career, you'll get used to it, and it won't seem like a burden. And if you treat law school like an 8–5 job, this won't *ever* feel like a burden; since you will be on-campus during the day anyway, you may as well attend all the daily meetings offered by the administration or career office.

While I could expand on how law schools could better serve or target their own students, I won't. It doesn't help to whine, and as adults, we are each responsible for our own level of commitment and interest. So go to meetings. Read your e-mails. Read campus postings. Attend guest lectures. An increased level of involvement cannot possibly hurt you; it can only serve to help, whether in your career search, your exam-taking skills, or your community of support.

One particular thing I learned about at a campus meeting (which I learned about through a campus e-mail) was volunteering. I happened to attend a lunch session where the career office presented a representative from a local legal clinic to speak about what the clinic did and how law students could get involved. I sat through the meeting, enjoyed my free pizza, and considered the possibility of volunteering with this agency. Not only would it allow me to learn some basics of lawyering (which, as a 2L, I lacked in every conceivable way) and spice up my résumé, it would also allow me to give back to my community, something that greatly appealed to me. I contacted the agency and thereafter joined their team representing indigent clients in personal and family matters.

When I came to law school, I never intended to practice. But after volunteering in a legal clinic for a year, my perception of lawyers and the practice of law was radically altered. Without that experience, I never would have seen this side of the law, and I never would have seen this side of the law had I not read my e-mail. Dramatic, but true. My volunteer work also led me to have a profound respect for community involvement as a lawyer. The practice of law can be very profit-driven, so much so that many students forget the basic mission of attorneys: *to help people.* And the best way to help people is to help the people who need help the most.

Even if that little plea doesn't tug on your heartstrings, there are practical reasons for choosing volunteer work. Finding a part-time job is fantastic, but there are not always enough jobs to go around. Additionally, part-time jobs can be more demanding of your time than volunteer work, which is inherently more flexible.

Now, let me throw in a quick note about "networking." "Networking" is probably the most overused, and therefore meaningless, word in law school (and maybe even in the legal field). If you're like most students, the word "networking" sends chills down your spine. While that word, and everything associated with it, may not appeal to you, its core concept is a fundamental part of your legal career. In order to start fresh and steer away from any of the pre-conceptions you have about "networking," let's give this concept a completely arbitrary name before espousing its benefits. Let's call it "seawalking."

Seawalking is basically the idea of getting to know people. Pretty harmless, right? Seawalking is something you need to learn and embrace, because the more people you know in your profession and in life, the better off you'll be. The larger your seawalk of individuals is, the more opportunities you'll be presented with in the way of jobs, recommendations, and social interactions. It is here that I will make quite possibly the boldest assertion in this book: **the only way to get a job is through seawalking.** That's it. It is tempting to think that your credentials will speak for themselves, but it is also naïve. Say you're applying for a summer job at a small firm. You and one other candidate have the same GPA, the same involvement in school activities, and the same work experience. No one at the law firm knows your name. Three partners have met Candidate 2 at the Annual Law School Seawalking Event, and two associates routinely see him at Volunteer Lawyers for Poor People events. Who do you think the firm will hire? Who would *you* hire? Maybe it's unfair, but that's the way it works. You want people to know you. People who know you and like you will want to help you. And having people on your side is the best thing you can do for yourself. Numerous professors have told us that the legal market is much tougher than when they were in school and the economic pressure much worse. With an increasing number of law school graduates every year, you need all the help you can get.

The reason I mention this is that volunteering is one of the best ways to seawalk in law school. Volunteer opportunities are abundant and, though it might be hard to believe, you *will* have enough time to take advantage of them. Since volunteering is more flexible than other commitments, you can choose to volunteer for twenty hours a week or two, and you can volunteer at a legal clinic or an elementary school. Think of the positives: you get real-world experience, learn a thing or two about life, meet local attorneys, and help the world. Not too shabby. Moral of this meandering story: volunteer, check your e-mail, and learn how to seawalk.

POST

20

Protect Yourself by Being Professionally Active

Elizabeth

"*My only ambition is to get a job that doesn't suck.*"

—2L

The annoying part about not knowing what you want to do when you graduate is that no one else knows either. A lot of students, myself included, have this idea of walking into a career counselor's office and being told exactly what to do in order to achieve professional contentment. This, apparently, is not the way it works. Guidance counselors and career centers are usually pretty good at answering specific questions and helping you with specific problems. But if you walk in to meet with a dean or professional faculty member and ask: "What should I do when I graduate and how do I get there?" you will hear a quick retort of "Well, what do you *want* to do?" followed by some generic advice about making good grades and checking the all-campus job postings. You will leave that meeting feeling more confused than when you arrived, hopelessly certain that if a professional can't help you, no one can.

One of the maddening aspects of the legal profession, and law school in particular, is the timing of certain job and internship applications; some opportunities will require you to apply over a year in advance while others will extend the opportunity only when an opening is immediately available. This means that you have to set goals for yourself pretty early on, in the event that you might actually be interested in one of the summer or post-graduation jobs with advance application procedures. There is nothing worse than finding your dream job, just to realize that the application deadline was yesterday.

This doesn't mean you have to set a path in stone for yourself right away. But you do need to be aware of *every* available career stepping stone so that you are able to choose from among the opportunities that interest you. You also need to be confident and, sometimes, just take a chance. I took the Foreign Service Exam, because it might lead me to a career I thought I would enjoy. I didn't know much about it, but I took a chance and signed up, knowing the most I could lose was a few hours on a Saturday.

A big part of being aware of every opportunity is reading campus announcements, including your e-mail, and attending on-campus informational sessions. And since I've already convinced you of the benefits of paying attention to communications from the law school, I won't be redundant.

A second way to familiarize yourself with different opportunities is by talking to professors: yet *another* way professors can help you. Merely having conversations with your professors, who have probably seen it all, and discussing your interests and abilities, will likely open your eyes to certain possibilities that were hidden before. I first heard about clerkships from a professor and was quickly convinced of their benefits. After this brief conversational introduction, I was able to research the topic on my own to learn about the application procedure and the job functions of a clerkship. Without my professor's suggestion, I would never have known that clerkships were something that interested me; I wouldn't even have known what they were.

Perhaps the most trusted method of researching career paths, however, is just researching career paths. Use your first semester of law school, and even before, as the time to find out what kinds of jobs are available to students and law graduates. Obviously, you will become an "attorney" upon passing the bar, but some students have no intention of practicing law, and many have no intention of practicing law at a firm. That's when independent research comes in handy. While a career office will do what they can to help, you will need to learn to carve your own path based on your own unique interests.

There are some pretty basic things you can do to make your career search and the interviewing process easier. First off, make sure you have a killer résumé. This doesn't just mean the content of your résumé—it also means the structure. I know it seems unimportant, but your résumé is a first impression, and you want your first impression to be memorable and professional. **Keep your résumé to one page.** A longer résumé can be acceptable if you have the experience to warrant it; if you are under the age of 25, you do not have that kind of experience. I know that making résumés is tedious and doesn't feel all that important. But a nice-looking résumé is worth it. We all have grand illusions of our capabilities, but realize that an employer will not spend thirty minutes reading your résumé. At best, you might get two. Make sure employers have everything they need to see right in front of them; make it as easy as possible for them to like you. Thus, the one-page rule. This might require that you create your résumé in something other than Word. You'll need a program that will allow for more layout flexibility, since you will want to take advantage of all the space on a page. If you need to, ask a friend for help.

Most employers will require a writing sample with your application packet. Be very strategic in the writing sample you select. The best writing sample to show an employer is a law review article, or a portion thereof. If you don't have one of these, use a paper from a class, a brief from any part-time work you've done, or something you've written in a legal internship. Be careful though; if you want to use a piece of writing that you did for someone else (i.e., as part of a job, either paid or volunteer), you will need to ask their permission first. You will also need to edit the sample to exclude any mention of client names or specific details. The least impressive writing sample you could include is a memo or brief that was assigned in a first year writing course. These will suffice if you have nothing else but they also show an employer that you have nothing else, and will need to be trained in practical legal writing. You want an employer to be confident in your ability to complete a project correctly.

Once you've selected a writing sample, carefully edit it so that it's not overwhelming for an employer. Again, let's not kid ourselves: employers will not spend an hour reading your legal manifesto. They don't have that kind of time, and they might be irritated that you thought they did. Select a section of your writing sample and condense it down to the greatest five to seven page writing sample they've ever seen. This is tedious and probably frustrating for you, but the likelihood of an employer reading a six-page paper is much greater than an employer reading a thirty-six-page paper. Take your chances if you must, but don't say I didn't warn you.

After your materials have been prepared and submitted, meet with a career counselor to go over interview strategies. Practice makes perfect. The most effective strategy for acing an interview is to **know your audience**. Research your audience. Dress, speak, and act appropriately. If you're interviewing with a firm, you should be able to list their biggest clients and know exactly what kind of cases they take. Find out the history of the firm and the names of the managing partners. If you're interviewing with a judge, know his most recent and most important decisions. Know the judge's past positions and current staff. Research the city in which you're interviewing if you don't live there. Just ask Kelsey about this one. During an on-campus interview with a firm her 2L fall, Kelsey went in blind, partially due to laziness and partially due to an unappreciation of how important preparation for an interview really is. She interviewed with a firm from Ft. Worth, Texas and spent the entire interview telling two partners how excited she would be to work in Dallas. Apparently, the employers were not too fond of this eagerness to work in an entirely *different city* than the one where their firm was located. Kelsey's elementary mistake came from a) not actually knowing where the firm was located and b) not knowing the difference between Dallas and Ft. Worth. Imagine telling a law firm in Brooklyn how excited you are to work in Manhattan—not very impressive. This kind of mistake is easy to make and might even stem from a habit or conversational slight. But this kind of mistake is also extremely detrimental; who wants to hire someone who has no idea what she's talking about? (In case you didn't already figure out the ending of this story, Kelsey was *not* offered a follow-up interview.)

Knowing what you're talking about will also be important when it comes to small talk. Come up with a reason for wanting to work at that specific firm or agency, in that specific city. Be convincing. When a law student admits she doesn't know exactly what she wants to end up doing or where she wants to end up working (which is a lot of the time), employers are not usually impressed. You will have time to learn to love your job, but an employer needs to love you immediately.

There is one exception to the what-kind-of-law-do-you-want-to-practice predicament, but it is most useful for internships, temporary full-time employment after graduation (like a one-year assignment), and bigger law firms. The possible alternative for pinpointing a career path is to admit to employers that you're not *entirely* sure what type of law you want to be practicing in twenty years, but you do know what you *don't* want to do (i.e., "I couldn't see myself being a transactional attorney")—just make sure the employer you're interviewing with doesn't exclusively do the thing you say you *don't* want to do. This works on a few levels: it shows an employer that you're open to many possible career paths, you are not apathetic and have an opinion on the legal profession, and no one can question your honesty or accuse you of professional superficiality. A 23-year-old who claims to know that he will only ever be an energy attorney and nothing else sounds more ignorant than driven. With no experience as an energy attorney, how can he possibly know? Honesty is key here. Never answer the inevitable what-do-you-want-to-do question with a mere "I don't know" and a smile. You should either answer with a real answer or answer with an extended reasoning for your *lack* of a real answer.

Before the interview, **come up with a list of out-of-the-ordinary questions to ask interviewers.** This does not mean *weird* questions. But when employers interview 20, 30, or 40 2Ls, how often do you think they hear questions like "What are the specifics of the partner track?" It will be much more interesting for them, and you, if you ask more natural and light-hearted questions, i.e., "What's the worst interviewing experience you've had?," "What is the best attribute a law student can have to succeed in this job?," or "What is *your* favorite part of your job?" These questions will likely lead to a more lively debate, which in turn will make you more memorable. Have a conversation with these people, because the ultimate goal is that they remember and like *you*, not your grades or extracurricular list.

Remember the names (first and last) of every attorney, judge, or employee you meet during an interview. Write them down after the interview if you have to. Hand-write thank you notes to each person and mail them (by snail mail, *not* e-mail) the day after your interview—no exceptions. Include in the thank you note something specific to the conversation you had during your interview. ("I hope you enjoy your weekend on the boat—it sounded amazing!" or "I hope to see you at the next race!") You would be shocked at how far little gestures go in making a good impression. Make a good impression.

These are all strategies to ensure that once you've *identified* your preferred opportunities, *you* get an opportunity to *secure* them. And this is all advice you can get from your school's professional development department or career counselor. But many law students expect someone to show them the light, so to speak. It's best to burst your optimistic bubble now. You are responsible for understanding and taking advantage of every job possibility available to you. Do not overlook this or wait too long to start looking. Your future is in your hands; take responsibility from the beginning.

21

Don't Sell Your Soul, Sell Yourself

Elizabeth

Imagine a world in which you are a 3L. Two and a half years of legal studies behind you. Birds chirping, sun shining. You have a good GPA, a solid network of attorneys in town, and a few internships under your belt. Sixty-three days to graduation, and nothing standing in your way. You start putting all your energy behind the job search. Not only do you send out what feels like thousands of applications, but you also start contacting people you know for a heads up on possible openings and opportunities. So far, you have done everything right. Just like the other 10,000 almost-lawyers looking for jobs. So, what makes *you* special?

An important component of being professionally proactive and succeeding in the job search is to set yourself apart from the crowd. Be distinct, and be memorable. If you can manage that, then people will remember you; *employers* will remember you. One way of setting yourself apart is with a high GPA and outstanding academic credentials. But that's not the *only* way. If you can count on being in the top 5% of your class, you already have an advantage that sets you apart from 95% of your peers. But just because you don't have an outstanding GPA doesn't mean you can't be an outstanding student, job applicant, or attorney. The trick is finding a way to present yourself that shows an employer and, in the future, a client that you are special. Give people a reason to take a chance on you.

Setting yourself apart can be accomplished in a lot of different ways. A good starting point is to do what interests you. Chances are *something* interests you and taking advantage of opportunities that you like will not only lead to much more enjoyable volunteer and work experience, but also to a unique perspective on the legal field. For instance, I did some work in immigration law while I was in law school, not because I thought it would look good on paper, but because I was interested in immigration law. I also volunteered at a local legal aid clinic because it was something that piqued my curiosity. And you know what? Taking advantage of the opportunities that interested me was what *made* me look good on paper. My select combination of experiences distinguishes me from my peers; I stand out and employers take note of my passion for certain areas of the law.

Which is not to say that I have cornered myself into one specific type of job. A law firm, government agency, or non-profit organization will not look at a résumé like mine and say, "Oh, your experience is too far removed from what we do." Rather, they will think, "What an interesting candidate. She clearly has a wide variety of experiences and is passionate about finding the right job and producing good work." The fact is, it's hard to know exactly what you want to do before you ever have a chance to practice law, which makes it even harder to say definitively what kind of lawyer you'll be. It is much easier, however, to identify the opportunities that sound interesting to you and weed out those that don't. Developing your own interests is what will make you more marketable in the end.

This doesn't mean that the interests you develop necessarily have to be in the legal field for them to be helpful. Specific skill sets will also lend a hand to making you a more marketable job applicant. Speaking a foreign language, for example, is essential for being considered for some jobs and certainly advantageous for many more. Unique skills narrow the candidate pool for jobs significantly, meaning you'll have a much greater chance of getting an interview, and an offer. If a national job posting lists fluency in Mandarin as a requirement for the position and you speak Mandarin, you should feel pretty confident that the application process will be much less competitive than the national job posting which simply requires a JD.

Law students have a tendency to undervalue their experiences, particularly if they aren't "related" to the law. Don't make this mistake. Just because you've never worked for a judge or clerked at a law firm doesn't make you a less attractive candidate for jobs, it just means you'll have to use other experiences to make a memorable impression on employers. I worked at an overnight summer camp as Program Director while I was in college. This sort of job is easy to overlook when you start building your legal résumé, but excluding it could be a mistake. Working at a summer camp, around the clock, every day, taught me to serve other people, work on someone else's schedule, and make sure every need was taken care of. Much like an attorney. Breaking up fights and directing alternative indoor activities when sudden downpours hit taught me instant problem-solving skills. Much like an attorney. A history of being a camp counselor won't be on every applicant's résumé; it's unique, and because of that, memorable. It also provides an interesting topic during interviews, which can be an invaluable asset.

Every life experience you've had sets you apart from all the other law school graduates and every experience has helped to shape your outlook and skill set. Use your interests, experiences, and skills to stand out from the crowd. Law school leads you to advocate on behalf of other people, but being a good advocate also means advocating for *yourself*, whether in the job search or beyond. Don't be afraid to sell yourself as a student or as an attorney, because if you show confidence and individuality, someone will buy your pitch.

22

Make It Rain

Kelsey

> "It's a little too corporate. I would rather do things my own way."
> —3L (who was not offered a position after a 2L internship)

> "It's good money, a great learning environment, a stable job, and the only way to really get my career started. Who wouldn't want that?"
> —3L (who was offered a position)

Almost everyone has an idea of what big law firms are like. If you've ever read a John Grisham book (or better yet, seen the movie), watched any courtroom drama (or dramedy, for Denny Crane fans), or heard any lawyer folklore, you've got a pretty vivid picture. They are the power suits, the safety-in-numbers, the outrageous legal fees, the brilliant strategists, and the people on the other side of the table from Erin Brockovich and the Rainmaker; they are the big firms.

Surprisingly enough, big firms are portrayed this way for a reason. Much of big firm life carries the characteristics of these carefully crafted fictions. There are, however, noticeable differences. I am not the expert on big firm cultures and practices throughout the country, so I won't attempt to stereotype, or de-stereotype as the case may be. Instead, I will submit that big firm life has broad advantages and disadvantages that probably ring true despite individual firm quirks.

The most obvious advantage to working as an associate at a big firm (at least to poor law students) is the salary. Large law firms usually pay their associates very well. While this invites criticism of industry-wide shockingly high legal fees, I wholeheartedly believe that associates at large firms earn their salaries. Big law provides a stable and usually beyond comfortable lifestyle, which can be very appealing when you have hundreds of thousands of dollars in student loans chasing you. And while as a student, or prestudent, this may be a primary motivating factor for choosing to take the big firm route, it is by no means the only advantage to big law. Not only will a large law firm provide you with potential wealth, it will also provide you with a *wealth* of information. (Corny, I know, but I couldn't resist.)

Baby lawyers will begin practicing with absolutely no real idea of how to actually be a lawyer. Knowing you have almost unlimited access to hundreds of experienced attorneys, dozens of examples of whatever it is you're assigned to work on, and your own research resources (including an in-house librarian if you're lucky) will make your first few years much less stressful in this regard. The resources of a large law firm are unparalleled, and this says a lot about how much experience you'll get. Your firm will train you thoroughly and well, because they are training you to work for them, and it's safe to assume that they only want the best to work for them. The value to you in this training is immeasurable and will increase your marketability whether you choose to stay at that firm your entire career or move elsewhere.

Of course, there are downsides to working at a large law firm. You will probably hear more negatives about big law than positives, depending on where you go to school, but it's undetermined how many of the people making these comments genuinely believe them, or are just making themselves feel better for not being accepted there. ("Oh, I *hate* big law firms. They're so impersonal," says the girl who couldn't get an interview. "Big law firms work you to death; I need a social life," says the guy who made it through his summer associate-ship without an offer of employment.) Nevertheless, there are pretty well-established characteristics of big law firms that are generally viewed as disadvantages, including the fact that you will have to work hard and work a lot. To some, this may be a plus, or at least an expected component of lawyering, but comparatively, a big law firm will generally require more hours logged than a smaller firm or government agency, at least right out of school. Big law firms rely on their associates and work them hard; it is not unmanageable, but do not expect to be home by 5, or even 6. You will work long hours, you may work weekends, and most importantly, you will be on someone else's (a partner's) schedule. During your first few years, you will not be given the opportunity to choose and manage your own caseload. Instead, you will be given assignments and projects to be completed according to someone else's timeframe. Which doesn't mean that you will be micromanaged or that your schedule will be completely inflexible, but your job will be to make your partners look good, if even to the detriment of your own agenda.

Another major misconception that doesn't translate from the movie perception of law firms is that, as a new associate, you will be sitting at a desk for the majority of your day. You will not be arguing cases in a courtroom every day, you will not be meeting new clients all the time, and you will not be walking through a courthouse like a big shot. You will be at your desk or in the library. You will research, and you will write. You may occasionally handle a deposition or two, and certainly, after enough time, you'll be given more responsibilities and see more action. But don't expect your first day or even year to be "exciting" in the ordinary sense of the word. You'll learn the nuts and bolts first—then you'll get to be a big shot. Expect that to take about ten years.

Big law firms usually do a substantial amount of recruiting. The prestige of your school will shape the schedule of on-campus interviews; top-ranked schools will draw in the largest firms from the largest cities, but even at lesser-known schools, larger firms in the area will generally recruit on campus. If you want to work at a big firm, try to get an internship for the summer after 1L year. You will apply and interview for these during your 1L spring after first semester grades have been released, although this partially depends on the firms you apply with. Summer internships for a 1L are pretty competitive and not as common as 2L summer internships, so don't be too disappointed if you can't find one: you're not out of the running yet. If you *do* land a job during the summer after your 1L year (which will be almost exclusively based on your first semester grades, as you won't have had much time to do anything else), then do a really good job. If they like you, they'll invite you back for the next summer and, hopefully, offer you a job after that. Not finding a big firm to take you on your first summer isn't the kiss of death. You can work at a small firm, study abroad, or take summer classes—anything with a legitimate relation to the legal profession. The important internship is the one after your 2L year.

Law firms (and law schools) are under pretty strict recruitment guidelines (created and enforced by NALP—the National Association for Law Placement). Schedule a meeting with your career office your first year to learn about the big firm hiring path and deadlines to apply, as these will be critical. Generally speaking, big firm recruitment will take place in early fall of your 2L year. For the firms that recruit on campus, the process is simple enough: submit the required materials through your career office and wait to be contacted about an initial interview. This interview will most likely be followed up by a second-round interview, which will be much more intense, scary, and exhausting. The firm will wine and dine you—that's the fun part, so enjoy it; it may not happen again. These firms will usually extend offers for summer internships in the middle of your fall semester, and you will have a certain amount of time to decide whether to accept. Each firm, and each smaller legal market, will have different rules about the length and timing of the internship (whether you can complete two six-week internships or just one, and whether you can choose to work the second-half or first-half of the summer), so check with your career office as soon as you know you're interested in working with a big firm.

If the firm or location you're interested in does not recruit on campus, you'll have to work a little harder. Coming from a smaller or less prestigious school will be a noticeable disadvantage in a situation like this, unless you have a strong personal or geographic connection to the firm. In all reality, a middle-of-the-road student from a small, lesser-known school in Louisiana probably doesn't have a shot at a summer job with a big firm in New York City. All this being said, it doesn't hurt to try. The summer after your 1L year, you should dedicate a week or two to preparing application packets, consisting of a cover letter, a résumé, a transcript, and a writing sample, at the very least. The key to this process is time: **make sure every cover letter is addressed to a specific person** (and make sure it's the *right* person), make sure your cover letter is specific to each firm and location, and make sure everything is done professionally. It will be very tempting to simply e-mail out your résumé, but how many e-mails do you delete on a daily basis? That's exactly what will happen to your hope for a summer job. As big of a pain in the ass as they are, I strongly recommend paper applications for almost any position; this forces a recruiter to actually see your name and glance at your credentials, something a PDF attachment won't always get you. (If you *are* sending out applications via e-mail, always, *always* make sure they are PDFs, not Word documents. If someone with a different program or different settings opens your application packet, the formatting may be totally screwed up. Then you will look bad, which is kind of the opposite of how this should work.) Mail your application packets out in late summer so that firms will have them before they make any decisions through on-campus recruiting.

The 2L interviewing season will be stressful. Prepare yourself. If you're lucky enough to receive more than one interview, you will likely feel like a commodity, moving from interview room to interview room and having the same conversation a hundred different times with fifty different people. You may interview with other students (the competition) or alone; both are equally uncomfortable. Keep your confidence up, and never stop smiling. The interviews will either go well, or they won't. Try not to put too much pressure on yourself to act natural, as this will certainly backfire. Be yourself, with some minor modifications if need be, and try to take a step back from the whole thing. Remember, you're interviewing the firms, too. If you're in a fortunate enough position, you will have your pick of all the firms you've interviewed with.

I interviewed with several different firms in the area, and I distinctly remember leaving one interview knowing that the firm had failed *my* initial test. The interview in question was one of many short meetings I had while I was at the firm interviewing (during the five-hour interview, I met with several different attorneys for a specified amount of time). I was sitting in the office of a young associate just a few years out of law school. He seemed cordial enough, and very friendly; interviews with younger associates are always less stressful than partner encounters, so I was fairly relaxed during this session. We started chatting, and he made a comment about the "problem" with women graduating from law school and joining big firms. I, being a woman, inquired further as to his meaning. He leaned back in his huge leather chair, posed perfectly in front of the floor to ceiling windows overlooking downtown, elbows out with fingers interlocked and holding his head, and responded with: "Well, they all just stop working to 'have babies' anyway, so what's the point?"

Now, I have never considered myself a feminist. I have never complained about my lot in life. In fact, I have always felt pretty equal with my male peers. But a comment like that really throws me for a loop. I felt like I had jumped back fifty years and needed to prove my worth to a second year associate at a law firm at which I didn't even work. And, believe it or not, this was the firm that had been bragging about its female empowerment program, designed to make women attorneys feel more comfortable. Needless to say, I felt less than comfortable at that firm and declined their offer for a summer internship.

Offers will come in pretty soon after you finish all your interviews. Strategy comes in to play here for some people; you may have to hold off on one offer while you're waiting to hear about another. Again, there are deadlines and rules associated with the offer process (promulgated by NALP), so you'll need to check with your career office and the firms themselves for the exact timing requirements of acceptance or rejection. I was fortunate enough to receive multiple offers after my interviews, which meant that I was able to pick and choose from the firms in my area. Knowing which firm I liked best based on my experience there, I was able to politely decline the other offers, some through polite though tense phone conversations, and some through handwritten letters.

Always be humble and courteous if you reject an offer of employment or even an invitation to interview. If you receive an offer to interview with an employer, and you know you will not accept an offer of employment if offered, decline the offer to interview. Otherwise, you waste your time, the employer's time, and deprive other law students of a potential opportunity. Employers let you down nicely, and you owe them the same. Although the entire situation feels competitive and contrived, almost every attorney you meet will be at least a decent person and an exceptional lawyer, and you will undoubtedly run into them all again at some point in your law school or professional career.

Once you've been offered a summer position, you'll be able to sit back and wait for summer. You will hear tons of horror stories about bad summer associates; many of them will be unbelievable, but true. In thinking of all the advice I could give you about how to succeed during your short time at the firm (which will be an extended, paid interview for a full-time position), it pretty much boils down to this: work hard. Really, really hard. Be the first one in the office, and the last one to leave. It's only a few weeks or months—it won't kill you. Leave your door open and accept **any** assignment someone is willing to give you. Be courteous and efficient. Ask good questions; it will make you look smarter. Don't wear headphones at your desk. Complete every assignment by the deadline you're given, or by the time you said you would have it done—no exceptions. Attend every social event and do not leave before the majority of the partners have; you need to show that you are dedicated to the firm and get along with the other attorneys. But, do **not** get drunk and make a partner take your car keys—no exceptions. Find the line between socializing and partying and do not, for any reason, cross that line. Do not cry at the office (at least where anyone else can see). Do not surf porn at your desk, and do not talk bad about **anyone** who works at the firm. Ever. Be exceptionally nice to the support staff. This will be impressive to the firm and is also a good overall life rule. You are not more important because you went to law school. You will never be. Above all, be smart and make smart, professional decisions. I know, pretty basic, but you'd be surprised.

Big law has a lot of perks, most of which will outweigh the cons. Start thinking about it now. Early preparation is the key to a well-laid path.

23

Some Lawyers Like a Small, Firm ...

Elizabeth

In fact, some lawyers *love* a small firm. Small firms are a pretty fantastic and flexible way to practice law. Whether you're in a tiny town of 100 or a crowded city of 100,000,000 small firms come in all shapes and sizes, ranging from one or two attorneys up to ten or twelve. Some firms have specialties, like personal injury, while some dabble in a bit of everything. The lifestyle of an attorney in a small firm is different than that of an attorney in big firm; expectations, hours, and support will likely differ dramatically.

One of the biggest benefits to working at a large law firm is the available support staff and resources. One of the biggest downsides to working at a small firm is the lack of these. It's entirely understandable: resources cost money, and as a general rule, big firms have more money to spend. It also stems from the number of attorneys at the firm; the more attorneys there are, the more guidance is available to you.

This doesn't mean a small firm is lacking in research or employs less qualified attorneys. All it means is that you, as a lawyer at a small firm, will have to be creative, efficient, and cost-effective in your research habits. You may end up back at your law school library while working on a client's brief, but that's okay; it's probably the most comprehensive legal resource in the area, anyway.

One of the main differences between small firms and large firms, and probably most important to law students, is the salary factor. We've already established that a small firm has a smaller expendable budget. They also have smaller salary budgets and cannot compete with large law firms in this department. But you're still a lawyer, and you will still make a good living. Depending on what type of firm you work for, how quickly you can make partner, or if you actually work for *yourself* at a small firm, the small firm path may even lead you to a greater financial bounty in the end. Just don't expect a starting salary to match that of an international law firm. Because it won't. Patience is a virtue, though, so try to focus on the other important aspects of the job.

One huge perk about life at a small law firm is the opportunity to deal with all sorts of legal problems. With fewer attorneys to go around, it's more likely that you'll be needed in a variety of areas, and not confined to one specific issue. Also expect quicker hands-on experience. Again, with fewer attorneys to go around, you'll likely be needed to step in and speak up in court much quicker than if you had fifteen supervising attorneys to take care of that for you. Additionally, because the number of "bosses" you have won't be overwhelming, expect more credit for the work you actually do. If vanity appeals to you, this is huge.

Perhaps the biggest perk of small firms, though, is the job flexibility. You will likely have a more flexible and less taxing schedule than a big firm lawyer. This is partly due to the fact that you have fewer partners to work for and partly due to the fact that the firm has less work in general. No matter what the reason, small firms are more accommodating to a greater variety of lifestyles. To many attorneys, especially those with more family or outside obligations, this is an invaluable benefit that cannot be ignored.

A good, albeit vague, method of finding employment at a small firm is to research your local legal market and start meeting attorneys. Again with the networking, I know. Professors can also be a good source for getting connected with small firms. Again with the professors, I know. But it's true. I found work at a small local firm while I was in school; the hours were convenient and the lawyers were very flexible with my schedule. I was able to work a few days a week while still carrying a full course load. The firm had contacted one of my professors, whom I had gotten to know through several classes, looking for a qualified law student to handle some research part-time. My professor notified me of the opportunity, and with his help, and recommendation, I got the job. That job allowed me to see the inner workings of a firm and perfect my research skills. If you do a good job for a firm, and don't burn any bridges, they might try to find a full-time home for you after graduation, which can be an ideal situation in a tough legal economy. If they don't have a spot for you, they will at least be willing to write you a good letter of recommendation or put you in touch with other small firms and solo attorneys who may be looking for help. If possible, try to get some experience with a small firm before you graduate. If nothing else, it will allow you to make note of what you like and what you don't. And, taken to its best, it's a proactive way to jump-start your post-grad job search.

24

A Law Student Walks Into a Bar …

Samantha

> "I didn't realize you couldn't just take 'the bar exam' and then go be a lawyer in any state. I definitely didn't know that any of them cost money. Couple of hundred dollars here, couple of hundred dollars there … it really adds up."
>
> —3L
>
> "Keep in mind that you'll be the most knowledgeable about the law the day you walk into the bar exam. Be confident in what you know, and realize that you can't possibly know everything."
>
> —Post-L
>
> "When you're studying for the bar, don't be afraid to ask for help. Don't have too much pride. You aren't competing against each other like in law school; you are all just trying to pass."
>
> —Post-L

The bar (exam, not drinking establishment). This is it—the culmination of three years of time and effort. And money. No pressure. You just have to pass the bar.[1]

The bar exam is the legal community's gatekeeper: it weeds out those who are supposedly unfit to practice law. If you pass the bar, you are well on your way to becoming a licensed attorney. If you

---

1. Brief history (or folklore) lesson: A railing in the courtroom separates the observers from those involved in the litigation—the attorneys, judges, and court personnel. Passing the bar is the rite of passage when you transition from an observer to a participant—you literally get to pass from one side of the bar (railing) to the other side.

don't pass, you'll have to try again, as you must pass the bar exam to practice law in any state.[2]

When I started law school, I knew the bar exam *existed*, but that's about it. I didn't know exactly what it was, or why I had to take it. Had I known these very basic truisms, I might have had a better idea of where I was headed, both literally and figuratively.

As logic may imply, you will need to apply to take the bar exam, which is a state-specific process. In other words, each state regulates the process by which its attorneys are tested, licensed, and otherwise deemed qualified to practice law. If you know or have an idea of where you want to take the bar exam, look into it early—it is essential to know your state's timeline for application and any other requirements that might be applicable.

You'll start hearing bar exam buzz as early as your first semester. Kaplan, BARBRI, and other companies will be on campus trying to get you to sign up for their respective bar review courses. Now, keep in mind, their pitches will be for something almost 3 *years* away; these are the review courses you will take immediately after graduation in preparation for the bar exam. If you know you will take a bar review course (and there's a 99% chance you will), there are benefits to signing up for the review courses early, even 3 years early, such as locking in a price (as it will inevitably increase by the time you reach your third year) and receiving some "free" study aids for your first year courses. You'll have to designate which state's bar review course you plan to take, thus you'll need to know which state's bar you think you'll take; this can, however, always be changed later.

Unless you're the elusive 1%, or Frank Abagnale,[3] you'll want to take a bar review course. There are a couple of options, and you'll

---

2. Unless you go to law school in Wisconsin, in which case you might be admitted to practice law without having to endure this dreaded ordeal. Otherwise, you're stuck.

3. The real life character portrayed, however loosely, in the film (and book) *Catch Me If You Can*, who in his youth made a career of impersonating a pilot, a doctor, and a lawyer, among others. He managed to pass the Louisiana bar without taking a course to prepare, or, for that matter, going to law school.

have a choice of companies and programs either way: a structured, "in class" bar review program or a self-study bar review program. If you know your learning style, this will likely be an easy decision. But as a basic rule, unless you *know* you can handle the self-study review, opt for the bar review course option.

Should you opt to take a self-study bar review course, you'll receive review materials including outlines, questions, and pre-recorded lectures, but it is up to you to learn the material. In other words, you will not attend a bar review class. Rather, you will learn the material on your own time and schedule. This option can be substantially less expensive, but it is only a good option for those who know they are disciplined enough to cover all of the material in an efficient manner. You need to be disciplined if you take this route, and you can't be afraid to ask for help.

One advantage to this approach is that you will remove yourself from the structured, albeit anxiety-ridden, review course environment. You won't be exposed to other people's anxieties and fears—at least not on a daily basis. But this might also be a disadvantage, as you will need to find people to reach out to for help, and you *have* to reach out for help. If you have a question, ask someone who is in a bar review course—they'll probably be willing to help. To repeat: **do not be afraid to ask for help from anyone who may be able to provide it.**

The classic bar review course is the best option for most people. You'll be provided with review materials much like a self-study program, but you will go to class each day for lectures (some live, some via streaming video) on bar topics. You'll learn, or at least be taught, everything you need to know for the bar exam in this bar review course and, periodically, you'll do practice exam questions and discuss bar exam-taking strategies. You won't just learn the material on which you'll be tested, but—just as important—you will learn *how* to take the exam, what you can expect to be on the exam, and tips and strategies on how to write or choose the best answer. Such guidance is invaluable.

While going to bar review class can arguably be considered studying, expect to put in additional hours studying outside of the structured classroom environment. With hundreds of thousands of dollars likely invested in law school, you might as well go ahead and do all that you can to ensure you'll pass the bar. The *first* time you take it.

Just like everything else we've discussed with regard to law school, the amount of time you'll spend studying for the bar exam will vary from student to student. Your law professors or bar counselors might imply, or even explicitly say, that you need to spend 18 hours a day studying for the bar. This *might* be true for some people. Maybe. But it might also be an unrealistic expectation. You have to do what you are comfortable with. You are the only person who will know whether or not you are learning the material. If it takes you 8 hours of studying each day, that's great. Maybe it will take you 12 hours of studying each day. There is no hard-and-fast rule as to how many hours of cumulative study will put you past that threshold of passing the bar, and—what's worse—you won't know how much is enough until you get the results. All you can do is put the time into it, ask questions, and be confident when you walk into the exam that you are prepared. What matters most is the *quality* of time you put into your bar review studies, not just the quantity.

The bar exam is offered twice a year—every February and July. However, the application process takes a considerable amount of time and effort, and you will have to start applying to take the bar far in advance of the actual test date. For the application, you'll basically need to know and disclose every identifiable detail about your life for the past 10 years, including those details you'd rather forget. Here's the basic rule: when in doubt, disclose. Trust me. Better to disclose that speeding ticket (or worse) from your spring break road trip sophomore year now rather than having to explain *why* you didn't disclose it later.

Some states have a bifurcated application process where you provide information to satisfy a character check, and then you apply to take the exam itself. If you're planning to take the exam in the same state where you attend school, you'll likely find that you have many more resources to help you through the process. This is by no means a discriminatory process, but merely a result of the faculty and staff being much more knowledgeable about their home state than one of the other 49. If you take another state's bar exam, plan on doing a lot of research on your own time. The bar exam is generally a two or three day comprehensive exam. Some jurisdictions will give you the option of taking the exam on a computer. There are several components (and combinations thereof) you could see on any state's bar exam: the Multistate Bar Examination, the Multistate Essay Examination, the Multistate Performance Test, and a state-specific portion. As of this writing, the Multistate Bar Examination (MBE) is a six-hour, 200 multiple-choice question exam covering criminal law, evidence, real property, constitutional law, torts, and contracts. Some states administer the Multistate Essay Examination (MEE), typically comprised of six 30-minute essay questions. In addition, most states also administer the Multistate Performance Test (MPT). The MPT generally consists of two 90-minute written exercises in lawyering skills. Here's the annoying part: *you* have to pay *money* to partake in all this fun. Can't you just hear the loans calling your name? If you take nothing else away from this, know that the bar exam is a long, intensive test that you need to pass in order to practice law. And you'll have to pay for it.

Expect the bar exam to be one of the most ridiculous test-taking experiences you will ever have. It is hard. **No one**, or at least no one normal, walks out of the bar exam feeling really great about it. Many will walk out despondent about life. Try to be the reasonable, rational person who falls somewhere in the middle of the continuum. Do all that you can to be confident in your preparation for the exam. Remind yourself that you prepared well and don't get caught up in the fretful atmosphere around you.

It's possible that a fellow exam-taker will ask if you have any Tums. You will witness violent pacing in the hallways prior to the exam. Loud sighs will reverberate throughout the exam room. Expect to see tears or—if you're lucky—a full-blown psychological breakdown. *You* might even do some or all of these things (try really hard to at least avoid visible tears and/or a public breakdown—wait until you get home if you feel like hurling your cell phone at a wall). Prepare yourself for these distractions; expect them. Take earplugs, inner peace, and a sense of humor.

In addition to the bar exam, all but four jurisdictions also require you to take and pass the Multistate Professional Responsibility Examination (MPRE) as a requisite to being licensed as an attorney. The MPRE is a 2-hour multiple-choice exam addressing ethical situations in which a lawyer might find himself. You can take this exam while you are still in law school—the best time to take it is soon after you complete your professional responsibility course. And, believe it or not, each state has its own minimum score requirements. Although the MPRE is administered nationally (not state-by-state), your score will need to satisfy the minimum score required by the state in which you want to practice law.[4]

The bar exam itself is overwhelming, but the application process might be just as bad. Look into your state's bar exam application process and requirements early: you'll get an idea of what you can expect when it comes time to apply to the bar and, hopefully, it will seem a little less overwhelming.

---

4. Say you get a 77 on the MPRE. You will be eligible to practice law in Alabama, as its designated passing score is 75. You will not be able to practice law in Utah, as its minimum passing score is 86. This is good (or at least acceptable) news if you applied to take the Alabama bar exam. This is bad news if you want to work in Utah. You will have to re-take the MPRE.

25

3 Years of L?

"Law school isn't rocket science. It more or less comes down to hard work and dedication."

—2L

"The old saying, 'first year they scare you to death, second year they work you to death, and third year they bore you death,' is completely true."

—3L

"You have to go out of your way to fail. Go to class. Be there. Be familiar with the concepts. Just by going through the motions, you should be able to get by with a C."

—3L

Law school isn't as bad as everyone makes it out to be. It really isn't. You might hate it sometimes, but that happens to everyone, everywhere, at some point or another. It's a big time commitment and a big financial commitment, but if you can get *into* law school, you can get *through* law school. Every now and then, just remind yourself of the important things in life and assure yourself that some things are beyond your control. Appreciate these three years for what they are, and what they aren't; hopefully you'll enjoy the journey, not just the destination. And assuming all else fails, try med school. Just make sure you know a good attorney.

Appendix 1

Our Unofficial Legal Dictionary

Kelsey

__ L: 1, 2, 3: Refers to your year in law school (1L is your first year, and so on). A student (you) will be called a "1L" and it will be referred to as "1L" year, or a "1L" class. I always thought the "L" stood for "Level," but it could very well mean "Law," "Lawyer," "Litigator," "Leftist," "Liberal" or "Lion" for all I know. It doesn't much matter, a 1L is a 1L any way you slice it. Equally important, a 3L is a 3L across the board, and *that* is something to look forward to.

ALWD (pronounced ALL-WOOD): Association of Legal Writing Directors. A style of citation. You will use either this or *Bluebook* in your legal writing class and on law review. It will become a giant pain.

Anonymous Exam Number: A number randomly assigned to you every semester so you can take your exam without your professors knowing whose is whose. This helps if you are the class asshole.

Bar Association: Your state will have a State X Bar Association, which is a group of attorneys who regulate the legal professional within State X. Along with taking the bar exam, in many states admission to the State X Bar Association will be a precursor to practicing.

Bar Exam: Didn't you read that whole chapter on it?

Bar Review: A very expensive set of classes you attend between graduation and taking the bar exam. The type and number you sign up for will depend on your state, but you will most likely take some kind of bar review course. Bar review companies will come on campus your first semester and nag you with offers and guarantee you a lower rate for signing up early and probably offer you some free supplements for your classes. I did not sign up my first semester because I was overwhelmed with the idea, and wasn't entirely sure what bar review classes were. Eventually, I did enroll (at a higher price tag, of course) because I wanted to pass the bar. You may as well enroll your first semester and try to save some money because there is a 99% chance you will eventually enroll.

BARBRI: A bar review test prep company.

Black's Law Dictionary: Buy one. Use it.

Bluebook: An alternate style of citation and style, although this one is more common than ALWD. This will also be a giant pain.

Bluebook: A thin journal with blank, lined pages inside that you will use to write an exam. This is literally a little blue book.

Briefs: Underwear. Also could refer to either a case brief or a legal brief.

A case brief is a method of dissecting a case in order to understand it (or, more importantly, to answer questions if called on in class) by creating a document that highlights the important points and language from the case. Many people suggest a variation of the IRAC method (Issue, Rule, Analysis, Conclusion). You will be able to find a lot of information on case briefs and how to write one, but they are not as essential as you think. If you can't understand a case, then by all means, make a formal brief in a separate document. But if you can read carefully, understand fully, and remember well, then it might not be worth the trouble. You will also hear about "book briefing" which essentially just means writing all over the case in your book and circling or highlighting the important language. No one method is best; the key is to read closely and understand the case. I never formally briefed a case, and I survived. Find what works for you.

A legal brief is a written document prepared for the court that argues a certain position in a case. These are common assignments in a first year legal writing class, and will require some amount of research and correct citation use. Your legal writing professor will most likely dictate the way your brief should be written. From my experience, this will not help you in a practical setting. Ever. A legal *memo* usually refers to a document an associate attorney will write for a partner or other attorney in his firm which analyzes the same type of legal issue, but is usually less argumentative and more focused on the current state of the law, the client's chances of winning, and potential strategies to be pursued. Your legal writing class may have you write a memo as well, but again, this probably won't help much when you get thrown into the real world.

Casebook: A textbook for a class. It has a bunch of cases in it.

Citation: Formal reference to a case, book, article, or anything really. There are a lot of citation rules (you might think you could just write down the case name, but you cannot. Shocking, I know). Whenever you write a research paper (or anything really), you will have to use cases, books, articles, or anything that supports your case. And then you will have to cite to them—which is when you will start learning the rules of citation. *See* **ALWD**, *Bluebook*, or **Law Review**.

Citation: A speeding ticket or other embarrassing legal problem. Keep track of these for your bar application. In the alternative, try not to get them.

Civil Law: A system based primarily on statutes and not case law. The idea of precedent, or stare decisis, is not as pervasive in these systems.

Clerkship: This usually refers to working for a judge and completing research assignments or helping to draft opinions. Almost all judges have some type of clerk. Federal clerkships (fixed-term positions with federal judges after graduation) are very prestigious and competitive positions which will do wonders for your career. Or so we've heard.

Common Law: A legal system where past cases are used as the rule for future cases (precedent).

Concurring Opinion: An opinion by a judge which agrees with the majority opinion (and consequently the rule of the court) but either has a different reasoning or just feels like saying something.

Dicta: The pages and pages of things judges sometimes write that have no bearing on the outcome of the case. Sometimes interesting, sometimes boring, this information will not be very helpful to you in the pursuit of figuring out the rules of law, as it has no precedential value.

Dissenting Opinion: A judge or justice who disagrees with a majority of the court will write a "dissent." Most of the time, you won't need to know what this judge wishes the rule were. But, sometimes you will need to understand her reasoning (in order to argue both sides effectively). It's relatively safe to assume you will need to read the dissent if it's included in some detail in your casebook. You will probably never need to brief a dissent. After all, there really is no rule that comes from it.

Fact Pattern: A hypothetical legal problem full of hypothetical facts. On an exam, the "fact pattern" is the essay question, describing the legal woes of a person, company, or community. These essay questions can be as long as several typed pages.

Fellowship: These are usually post-graduate positions and may be with a non-profit organization, government agency, or university. They are fixed-term positions (usually one or two years) that come with a stipend (salary) and involve working in a research capacity. If you like to research and write, look into these opportunities. Many of them will provide flexibility in developing your own fellowship based on something you are specifically interested in. Ask your career services office for help.

Foreign Service Exam: An exam offered by the government for eligibility as a Foreign Service officer. It's free to take, but requires a pretty lengthy application and background report. The exam is the first step in becoming part of the Foreign Service; there are narrowing procedures after passing the exam, including personal interviews. Do some research or check with your career counselor about when you can take it and where it will take *you*.

Grading Curve: Many law schools institute a mandatory grading curve for first year classes. That means professors can only give out so many As, so many Bs and so on. It is both comforting and disturbing to realize that your performance is not viewed in isolation but is graded in relation to other students. So do the basic first year test: in any class, look to your left, look to your right, then write a better exam than either of those people.

Hairiness: An automatic spell-check correction for "hahahaha." This will be important when chatting online/texting in class. You will accidentally say "hairiness" when referring to the class asshole. This could be bad for you. You're better off taking Samantha's advice and leaving your computer at home.

Hornbook: To be honest, I don't really know. Some sort of cross between a textbook and a treatise. A hardback book in the library that helps explain things you learn in class. A supplement of sorts (*see* **Supplement**). This seems to be an antiquated term—I've never heard a student *ever* use this word. Next.

Igor: A person you meet on spring break. Yes, there are spring breaks in law school. Yes, you can do something fun. No, you won't have to study during spring break. I have heard of people who spend their spring breaks studying, but I have *no* idea what they're actually doing. You can take a week-long cruise, or a 9-day road trip, and still make As.

Inns of Court: A networking group comprised of local attorneys, judges, professors, and law students. You will have to be accepted as a member, and it's a pretty structured group. Each member has a designation within the group, and the focus is on perfecting litigation and advocacy techniques. None of the authors of this book know anyone who was involved in this.

Jury Nullification: When a jury decides to ignore the law and votes someone guilty/not guilty despite the evidence or the law.

Law Journal/Law Review: A student-run scholarly publication. You should have read about this already.

Legal Clinic: This is not where you go when law school drives you crazy—that's called a bar. This is a law-school run, non-profit "law firm," usually to benefit a specialized group of less fortunate individuals (for example, an immigration clinic). Legal clinics offer great practical experience for students, and you usually get class credit for working there.

Legal Fraternity: This is not like a real fraternity, but more like an organized group of people who get together and do things.[1] These can be fun, but aren't essential; they're a good way to get to know people and do positive things for the community. They're also helpful to talk about in a job interview as an example of community involvement and work ethic if you a) take an active role or b) are okay with editorializing your involvement. But be aware: I've never heard of an employer bonding with an applicant because of a mutual membership in a legal fraternity. Look for various types of legal fraternities (a social one vs. a scholarly one, for example), although this probably won't make a difference. If you decide to join one, **pick the one with the most interesting and fun people**, because that's really the whole point.

Legal Intern: You'll hear the term "legal intern" thrown around for almost any job a law student gets. After all, you're probably interning and it's probably in the legal field. Hence "legal intern."

There is such a thing as a "Licensed Legal Intern," however (although this depends on what state you're in). A licensed intern has a limited license to practice law, and the license is governed by the state bar association. In very limited circumstances, this license allows law students to appear in court and handle certain parts of litigation. There are some pretty heavy requirements to obtain one of these licenses, like passing the MPRE and taking a multiple-choice exam specific to the license itself. Once you obtain a license and start using it, you'll likely have to report everything to the bar association, and there may be strict limitations on what you can and can't do and how or if the license expires. I'm sure this is beneficial experience. From what we've heard, though, it takes up a lot of time and a lot of effort, and it's not always worth the hassle.

LexisNexis: A legal research firm. You will come to know "Lexis" as an online research portal used to look up cases, secondary sources, statutes, etc.

---

1. The main difference is the coolness factor. No one has ever made a law school fraternity movie.

LLM: An advanced law degree. I know, I know—it's hard to imagine you can just keep getting law degrees. But you can. Getting an LLM after your JD will be useful if you want to specialize in something difficult (like tax law) or if you want to become an academic. LLMs are also used by graduates of foreign law schools in order to be eligible to practice in the U.S.

LSAC: Law School Admission Council. This is the comprehensive website you will use to prepare and submit law school applications, as well as the administrator of the LSAT.

Kaplan: A test prep company. You may use it to prepare for the MPRE, but more likely just for bar review classes.

Majority Opinion: The rule of the court.

Minority Opinion: An opinion of less than half of the court (i.e., *not* the rule).

Moot Court: Mock trial.

MPRE: Multistate Professional Responsibility Exam. Every state (or almost every state) requires it for admission to the bar, and each state has a different minimum score. It won't take up too much time; usually self-study will be sufficient. If you can manage to take it during or right after your school-mandated professional responsibility course, that will help.

Nutshell: A small book providing a very brief overview of a course or area of the law. Similar to a supplement. If you have no idea where to start, start with a nutshell.

OCI: On Campus Interview. Usually only the bigger employers will offer this, and typically there's a minimum GPA or other narrowing requirement in order to sign up.

Opinion: In the case of a judge, opinion means rule. When the majority of the Supreme Court issues an "opinion," it's a rule. At least until another "opinion" changes it.

Outline: There was a whole section on this. *See supra* Chapter 9: *How to Outline*. (There's a good lesson in citations for you.)

Pocket Constitution: You will most likely be handed several free versions of this during your first semester, usually from a bar review company, test prep company, or any other company trying to sell you something you undoubtedly "need." They are exactly what they sound like: tiny little Constitutions. These will come in handy during your Constitutional Law class, or on an exam. Keep at least one of these; it will prevent that embarrassing moment when you can't remember where to find the guaranty of freedom of speech in the Constitution.

Pocket Part: An update to a research book. Also, a punch line to many law school jokes.

Precedent: Cases that have been decided in the past on a certain issue in the same jurisdiction will become the binding rule. So if your case has already been argued before this same court and your argument lost, it is more than likely you will lose. There are some rules and exceptions, but for the most part, courts will have to follow precedent.

Reporters: Books that report and reprint cases decided in certain U.S. courts. Pay attention in your legal research class.

Restatement: There is a group of academics somewhere who sit around and decide what the law should be and how it should operate. Then they write it all down according to topic, and that becomes a "Restatement," like the Restatement of Torts. This is a good place to find secondary research and point you in the right direction, but it isn't technically the law.

SCOTUS: Supreme Court of the United States. Sounds nerdy, but helps with shorthand note-taking.

SJD: Another advanced law degree?! These seem to be pretty rare —I have never met anyone with an SJD. Usually you get it after your LLM, and if you want to be a professor or the best SCOTUS justice in all the land, then look into it.

Socratic Method: A "teaching" method in which professors take the liberty to call on you at their discretion, put you on the spot, ask convoluted questions, and generally humiliate you. Just pray your professors don't make you stand at the front of the class to answer.

Status Skank: The serial relationshipper who jumps from one "relationship" with fellow classmates to another. Every time this person updates their official online status, the entire school will wonder if it's a joke. It is not. This person really is that skanky.

Subciting (Cite-checking): This is a dirty word to every member of law review. Subciting entails taking another person's scholarly, legal article and checking their every last footnote. This doesn't sound too bad, until you realize that there will be hundreds of footnotes in a single article, each pointing to an entirely different source. You will then have to locate that source (however hard to find it is) and verify the accuracy of the footnote. Repeat three hundred times. This is the most tedious part of law review, but it's also the part that seems to have found a pretty stable home among legal journals.

Supplement: A book designed to help you learn the material easier than your textbook. It's usually less detailed and has a lot fewer cases, but it helps give you the big picture and sometimes will give you practice questions. For some classes a supplement won't help; for some classes, supplements are essential.

Textlationship: For the young, single law students, take careful note. The most common "dating" relationship you will have during law school (heck, maybe even during life) will be via a continuous string of text messages. Expect back-and-forth text conversations to last days, weeks, or months, without any physical or even vocal communication as a supplement. Call it progress if you want, but be prepared to sit at your desk all night, with your textbook, waiting for the next text ping. If nothing else, these textlationships (with the person you are textlating) will be good for a study distraction.

Textpert: You will be given this title if you can sit on the front row of a class in which technology is banned (i.e., no laptops), and keep in constant communication with your slacker friend on the back row.

Treatise: A really big book which supposedly explains legal concepts in a way that is more conducive to understanding. There are tons of different treatises covering every topic you can think of. I have never used one of these to help me understand something in a class, but they will help with legal research when it comes to writing your memos or briefs.

Westlaw: Another legal research company. You will come to know "Westlaw" as another online research portal. Westlaw and Lexis both have perks, but it really comes down to which you like better and which you are given access to.

Appendix 2

What *Omnia* Else Means (Our Unofficial Latin Dictionary)

Samantha

You might be wondering why we would include a *Latin* dictionary. While it is far less informative or useful than our *regular* unofficial dictionary, it will be helpful to have some knowledge of these terms before reading your first case—or at least to know that they exist and that you will see them frequently. If nothing else, you'll be able to nonchalantly explain what *stare decisis* means on the first day of orientation. And that's kind of a big deal.

Amicus curiae: No, not any sort of fungus or mold or contagious disease—much more genial than any of those things. Literally "friend of the court." An "amicus brief" is when a person or group (other than one of the parties to the litigation) offers his/its opinion as to why the court should rule a certain way. This third party believes that the court's decision will affect its interests in some way and wants to argue the benefits or consequences of a certain decision (often by invoking societal or policy concerns).

Certiorari: A writ of certiorari (cert). This is the method by which the Supreme Court of the United States (SCOTUS) decides to hear a case. It is a discretionary right used almost exclusively by the Supreme Court. A petitioner will appeal to the Supreme Court with a writ of certiorari. If four of the nine justices want to hear a case, for whatever reason, the court "grants cert" and will hear the case. Some state courts employ similar methods for granting review of a case under the guise of some other terminology (writ of review, leave to appeal, etc.).

In rem: The really deep sleep you'll fall into right before your alarm goes off. Kidding. Literally means "in a thing." This is a jurisdictional term referring to property (as opposed to personal disputes like a personal injury). When title to a piece of property is in dispute, an *in rem* action will determine the rightful owner.

In personam: Also a jurisdictional term. This is the type of legal action you probably envision when you think of a lawsuit. It pretty much encompasses everything that is not *in rem*—which is most things.

Mens rea: A guilty state of mind. You will see this term in your Criminal Law class. Simply put, it refers to one's state of mind when committing a crime (i.e., did a person have the requisite *mens rea*?).

Omnia: "Everything." Clever, huh? You will not come across this word in law school.

Per curiam: This is an opinion issued by an appellate court consisting of multiple judges. Normally, an opinion is written by one judge and may be joined by one or more of the remaining judges, but a *per curiam* opinion is basically an anonymous opinion by the court (at least a majority of the judges) whereby no single judge is credited with writing the majority opinion. Oddly enough, though, individual judges do write and sign concurring and dissenting opinions in a *per curiam* opinion situation. A curious legal concept.

Prima facie: This means that something (a piece of evidence) will be accepted as correct until it is proven incorrect by the opposing party.

Pro bono: For free. Like when an attorney is working "pro bono."

Pro se vs. per se: These two terms are unrelated—so there's no real reason they should have to go head-to-head. They look similar, though—enough to cause some confusion. *Pro se* is when a litigant doesn't have a lawyer and represents himself (like when a criminal defendant declines appointed counsel and proceeds *pro se*). *Per se* means "by itself," and you will talk about *negligence per se* in your Torts class.

Stare decisis: This might be the most important of the Latin terms. This simply means precedent. A court is obligated to follow the law emerging from the courts above it.

Sua sponte: When the court (a judge) raises an issue on its (his) own, and not on a motion from one of the parties. This is used in fairly limited circumstances—mostly with regard to jurisdictional issues—as courts usually prefer to stay out of the procedural spider web.

Voir dire: Technically this isn't Latin, but we didn't make a French dictionary, so you'll have to deal with it here. This is process by which a jury is chosen. Both sides are given the opportunity to question the pool of potential jurors and essentially weed out people they think won't be sympathetic to their side. *Voir dire* is substantially more complicated than it sounds, and can be a forum for intense controversy. Also, I don't know that there is really any consensus on how to pronounce this one—so you may sound like an idiot the first time you have to say it. Have fun in Civil Procedure.

Appendix 3

Careers

Sometimes, a student has no idea what he wants to "do." Welcome to *our* lives. Sometimes, though, a student *does* know what he wants to do with his law degree, but just doesn't know how to get there. It would have been immensely helpful to us if, at the beginning of law school, someone had laid out a few different examples of career paths, so we could start making choices and getting the right kind of experience. Certain jobs have very specific prerequisites, and usually these choices have to be made pretty early on. So if you do have a desire to work in a specific field, you should understand the different avenues necessary for that career path as soon as possible.

We have tried to break down different careers and pinpoint the important experiences and timing requirements associated with them in an attempt to give you at least a general idea of what you should be doing and when. Again, use this as a rough guide. We are, after all, students ourselves. After this brief review of certain careers and your own research, you should schedule a meeting with a career counselor at your school to get exact deadlines and information on any opportunities peculiar to your location or chosen field.

Big Firm Corporate Lawyer

- 1L Fall: Make the best grades possible.
- 1L Spring: Sign up for on-campus interviews with firms.
- 1L Summer: If you can't get an internship with a firm, do anything else law-related. Working at a small firm is particularly beneficial. Make and send out application packets to all the firms you are interested in who don't participate in OCI.
- 2L Fall: Join law review. Sign up for on-campus interviews. Interview. Do well. Juggle offers.

- 2L Spring: Don't fail.
- 2L Summer: Work as hard as you've ever worked for one summer. Impress the firm(s). Juggle offers.
- 3L Fall: Accept offer.
- 3L Spring: Try not to gloat. Don't fail.

Federal Government Attorney

- Research (**as soon as possible**) all of the government honors programs targeted at law students that offer summer or semester programs, or post-graduate positions, including:
  - Attorney General
  - Department of Commerce
  - Federal Trade Commission
  - Internal Revenue Service
  - Federal Communications Commission
  - Department of Justice
  - Department of Homeland Security
- Try to get work with a non-profit organization that mirrors the type of government work you'd like to do.
- Try to get a job with your city or state government agencies for experience.
- Take *any* government position you are offered, even if it's in a slightly different area than you had hoped; you will have a better chance of transferring within the government than getting a foot in later.
- Don't get arrested during law school.

Judicial Clerk

- Try to find internships with law firms during your summers.
- Join law review.
- Publish an article for law review.
- Intern with a local judge, either for credit or as a volunteer, during any semester.
- Apply for full-time, post-graduation clerkships during your 3L summer and fall.
- Don't limit your applications (some students submit *hundreds* of applications).

- Don't limit yourself (be open to *any* clerkship you can find).
- Don't give up: re-apply once you're out in practice.

Small Firm Lawyer

- Try to find internships with any firm over your summers.
- Network, network, network!
- Take advantage of any opportunity to get to know local attorneys.
- Join the local bar association and participate.
- Use your university's alumni connections to find opportunities.
- Work for a firm part-time during your 2L and 3L years if possible.

In-House Counsel

- Select a school carefully. Try to find one with corporate ties or donors, or in a city where you can find a corporation you are interested in.
- Research large corporation summer law internships early in your 1L year. Deadlines to apply can be up to a year in advance.
- Chances are you won't find an in-house position straight out of school, so go the big firm route.

Non-Profit Attorney

- Look for law schools with specific programs or clinics related to your interests.
- Do legal aid volunteer work while in law school.
- Try to get a part-time job with the local public defender or other experience with low-income clients.
- Start researching fellowships early on, and try to find one that might be a good fit.
- Do any type of volunteer work, either through the law school or on your own.
- Join student organizations and bar associations related to your chosen field.
- Network, network, network!

Criminal Attorney
- Take all the applicable courses (Criminal Procedure, Adjudication, etc.).
- Try to find part-time work with the public defender or prosecutor while still in school.
- Research local criminal firms and try to find a summer internship.
- Some cities have very competitive public defender internships; do your research early.
- Join the criminal division of your local bar association.

Professor/Academic
- Make good grades.
- Join law review.
- Get an article published.
- Perfect your legal writing (publishing articles is *very* important).
- Think about applying for LLM and SJD programs.
- Try to get a fellowship.
- Try to clerk for a judge (heck, try to clerk for a Supreme Court Justice).
- Network with professors and deans.
- If you go straight from school into practice, be sure to keep writing and publishing articles.

Artist Bum
- Practice living off of ramen noodles (oh, wait, you're a law student—you're probably pretty good at that already).
- Move to New York City, glue a bunch of hair on the wall and tell people it represents humanity's struggle for equality or the anger of underprivileged Asian schoolchildren.
- Frame your law diploma on the wall of your artist's studio.

Appendix 4

Basic Tutorial on U.S. Court Structure

If you were a PoliSci major in college, and if you're reading this book there's a 92%[1] chance you were, you won't need any lessons on the basics of the U.S. court system. But for the rare anomaly of a student who is attending law school with an art degree, you may need a starting point, or refresher course, on the basic structure of our judicial system. Although the judicial system is infinitely more complicated than this little sketch, it helps to know the basics before you start learning the specifics. So, for now, just take note that there are two, completely separate court systems in the U.S.: state and federal. Each system works at the same time, and one does not (usually) get to boss the other one around. The one link between the two systems is the U.S. Supreme Court, although it too only gets the final say on federal (Constitutional) matters, not matters of state law.

---

1. We made this up. But it sounds accurate.

APPENDIX 4

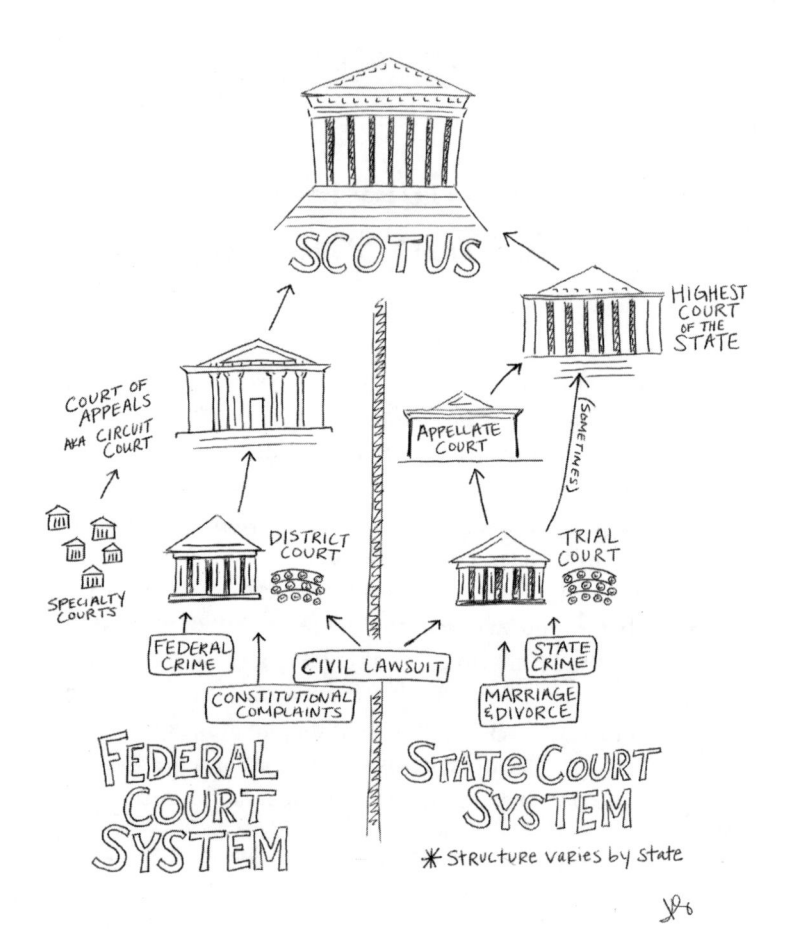

Federal Court System

- **SCOTUS**
- **Court of Appeals aka Circuit Court**
- **District Court**
- **Specialty Courts**

Handles: Federal Crime, Constitutional Complaints, Civil Lawsuit

State Court System
*Structure varies by state

- **Highest Court of the State**
- **Appellate Court** (sometimes)
- **Trial Court**

Handles: Civil Lawsuit, State Crime, Marriage & Divorce

Appendix 5

Sample Outline

DISCLAIMER: This outline should not be used for substantive law purposes, but merely as an example of layout and formatting.[1]

I. § 1983 for Constitutional Violations
   A. Cause of Action
     1. § 1983 creates a cause of action, jurisdiction comes from federal question jurisdictional statute; purpose is to protect people from unconstitutional acts by the states
     2. Elements:
       a) Person
         (1) NOT a state
         (2) *Maybe* a municipality
       b) Under color of state law
         (1) State actor requirement
       c) Causation
       d) Deprivation or loss under US Constitution
         (1) Need INTENT, not negligence
     3. CASE CITATION
       a) Case details
       b) Case rule
     4. CASE CITATION
       a) Case details
   B. Immunity
     1. Absolute
       a) Prosecutors have absolute immunity for prosecutorial functions

---

1. The substantive information could very well be wrong. But, since you've never been to law school, let's assume you won't know the difference. Therefore, we can assume it is all correct. Just don't sue us if you try to use it on an exam. To that end, do not try to use it on an exam. This is about 1/5 of the actual outline. It should be enough to give you an idea of what they look like and how to make one.

(1) Absolute immunity from damage suits for prosecutorial functions, but NOT from investigative functions
b) Judges have absolute immunity in judicial capacity, but NOT for administrative functions (like firing a clerk)
c) Legislators (state and local) have absolute immunity from damages and injunctive suits from legislative functions
d) President is absolutely immune from suit while in office
e) Police serving as witnesses are absolutely immune
2. Qualified
a) This is protection to officials in suits for damages; affirmative defense
b) **Governmental officials protected from damage suits if their conduct did not violate clearly established statutory or constitutional rights that a reasonable person would have known**
(1) What is clearly established?
(a) Would a regular person think this behavior is inconsistent with general principles?
(i) Obvious
(b) Need a case on point
(i) "Fair notice"
C. Municipalities and Counties
1. **Must show custom or policy in one of 5 ways:**
a) **Actions based on an official municipal policy**
b) **Actions by agencies or boards that exercise authority delegated by municipal legislative body**
c) **Individual with final authority to make decisions—Final Decisionmaker**
d) **Government policy of inadequate training, supervision, or hiring**
(1) Test: where failure to train, as a deliberate choice, evidences a "deliberate indifference" to the people's rights
(a) Training failure=deliberate indifference
(i) What is deliberate indifference?
(a) Failed to train in light of reasonable, foreseeable consequences
(b) Failed to train when recurring problem or after a pattern of problems emerge
e) **Custom sufficient to establish liability**
(1) Comes from bottom up
(2) Test: attributable to municipality, high-ranking officials knew about it, or should have known, and didn't stop it
(a) So widespread that municipal officials had actual or constructive knowledge
(b) And didn't stop it
(c) Causal connection

II. Habeas Corpus
A. 28 USC § 2241—allows federal judge to issue writs
B. 28 USC § 2254—deals with state prisoners, federal judges can order release of state prisoner
C. 28 USC § 2255—applies to federal prisoners—you ask for "2255" but it's the same effect as habeas (also has a safety clause to ensure its exactly like habeas)
D. Developed as a tool to compel attendance at a court proceeding
E. Biggest issue: how/when can Congress suspend the writ?
F. Constitution says=writ can only be suspended for rebellion or public safety (suspension clause)
   1. Only CONGRESS can suspend the writ
   2. If Congress wants to suspend the writ, it has to be clear and express
G. Does the habeas statute confer a right to aliens in US territory? Yes!
H. Habeas also extends to US citizens overseas and held by multi-national forces
I. **Habeas challenges to state convictions**
   a) All federal claims can be brought in habeas review when all state remedies have been exhausted
   b) Prior state court judgment does not preclude federal habeas review of federal claims
   c) De novo review over questions of law and questions of law + fact
   d) **You cannot raise an exclusionary rule you've already raised AND cannot raise new rules of law**
   e) New Rules of law
      (1) **Teague**
         (a) New rules of law are retroactive ONLY to cases on direct appeal
            (i) **New rules of criminal procedure apply to all cases in direct review**
         (b) Cannot raise issue that would be a new rule of law in habeas **UNLESS**:
            (i) Some sort of privacy the state cannot restrict (private conduct outside the power of the court to proscribe)
               (a) Class of people who cannot be executed
               (b) New rule of substantive law (like interpreting a federal criminal statute?)
            (ii) A bedrock of ordered liberty, watershed rule of law without which the accuracy would be questioned
               (a) *This has never occurred*
         (c) When is a rule "new"?
            (i) If precedent at the time the conviction was final wouldn't have compelled the decision

                (ii) OR breaks new ground
                (iii) OR imposes new obligations on the state
            (d) Final conviction is either SCOTUS denial of cert or the lapse of the 90 day filing period
    f) Standard of Review: §2254(d)(1) standard under **Terry Williams**:
        (1) Contrary to, or
            (a) Applies a rule that contradicts established law
            (b) Applies established rule to an indistinguishable set of facts
        (2) Unreasonable application of
            (a) Applies law unreasonably
            (b) Wrong is NOT necessarily unreasonable
            (c) Objective standard
        (3) Established law
            (a) If SCOTUS has already decided the issue and that law existed during the direct appeal
        (4) As set by SCOTUS
    g) Custody Requirement
        (1) Prison or on parole
        (2) Fines are NOT custody
    h) Exhaustion Doctrine
        (1) Must exhaust all available state remedies
        (2) And "fairly present" all of your claims in state court
            (a) Must raise it explicitly as a federal claim
        (3) Total Exhaustion Rule
            (a) All claims in habeas petition must be exhausted
            (b) If a mixed claim, the options are:
                (i) Go forward with exhausted claims
                (ii) Drop petition, go back and do them all, then bring it again
                (iii) Court could stay the petition, and petitioner could go back and exhaust
    i) Procedural Bar
        (1) Only way to get around valid bar is to show cause and prejudice (i.e., ineffective counsel) or if you show a fundamental miscarriage of justice (i.e., factual innocence)
    j) Standard of Review
        (1) Fed. Ct. can only grant relief on the merits if state decision was 1. Contrary to or 2. Unreasonable
    k) Statute of Limitations
        (1) 1 year from expiration of direct review, 90 days if no cert. petition is filed, or denial of cert if one is filed, or when SCOTUS affirms after accepting cert

(2) Statute tolled during a properly-filed post-conviction, but tolling does not include the cert. process after post-conviction
l) Evidentiary Hearings
  (1) §2254(c)(1)—deference a federal court has to give to state court finding of fact
  (2) Shall NOT hold evidentiary hearing unless:
    (a) Based on new rule, or
    (b) The facts could not have been previously discovered with due diligence AND but for the new facts a reasonable juror could not have convicted
m) Appellate Review
  (1) No appeal of right
  (2) Must petition the Court of Appeals
  (3) Looking for denial of significant, substantial showing of Constitutional violation
    (a) Satisfies standard when jurist of reason could disagree on the issues, or reasonable jurist could conclude that issues are adequate to deserve further review
n) Successive Appeals
  (1) 28 USC §2244
  (2) Can only be filed if:
    (a) Permission from Court of Appeals (cannot then appeal their decision for permission)
    (b) Presumption of not getting it—only if claim relies on retroactive rules of law or facts that couldn't have been discovered AND but-for causal conviction with clear and convincing evidence
o) §1983 and Habeas
  (1) Under §1983, prisoner can sue if terms/conditions of confinement violate Constitution
  (2) Prisoner cannot use §1983 to shorten or end confinement
  (3) Sole remedy for length of sentence is habeas
  (4) §1983=ONLY for conditions
  (5) If §1983 plaintiff is alleging something unconstitutional that calls the sentence into question, he must show the conviction was reversed on appeal, expunged, declared invalid, or was granted a habeas writ

Appendix 6

Sample Issue Map[1]

Mini-outlines, or "issue maps," specific to certain legal issues within a class, can be used to supplement a class outline, or can be used in place of an outline. They are most helpful when used to provide a structure from which to base your essay answer. Make a short list of rules and issues for every major theme in the class (expect maybe 4–5 of these in a particularly substantive class).

When writing your exam answer, follow the topics or questions in the checklist point by point, and that way, you'll ensure you don't miss anything. Even if the facts in the question don't implicate a certain part of the checklist, make sure and note on your exam that that particular rule of law doesn't apply. You don't want a professor to think you merely *forgot* an issue, as opposed to ruling it out as inapplicable.

II. Habeas Corpus
    A. Statute of Limitations
        1. 28 USC § 2244(d)(1)
        2. 1 year from final conviction (starting at denial of cert., lapse of time, or SCOTUS granting cert and deciding something else)
    B. Custody
        1. 28 USC § 2254(a)
        2. Prison or parole
    C. Exhaustion
        1. § 2254(b)-(c)
        2. Total Exhaustion
    D. Procedural Bar
        1. *Wainwright*
        2. Only get around this if:

---

1. Same disclaimer as before.

    a) Cause and prejudice (ineffective counsel), or
    b) Fundamental miscarriage of justice (factual innocence)
E. Teague
    1. §2254(b)(2)
    2. §2254(d)(1)
F. Standard of Review (Merits)
    1. §2254(d)(1)
    2. *Williams*
    3. The state judgment must be:
        a) Contrary to existing law, or
        b) Unreasonable
G. Evidentiary Hearing
    1. §2254(c)
    2. Only if:
        a) Based on new rule of law, or
        b) The facts could not previously have been discovered with due diligence AND a reasonable juror could not have convicted if the new facts were presented
H. Appeal
    1. §2253(c)(1)-(2)
I. Successive Hearings
    1. §2244
J. §1983 and Habeas
    1. *Prieser*
    2. *Heck*

Appendix 7

Sample Exam Answer

Kelsey

*We thought it would be helpful to show you what an actual student exam answer looks like, so you can get a feel for the style of writing and the format of an answer. We did not include the question, because this shouldn't be a lesson on the law. In fact, do **not** take this as a lesson on the law because, well, I wrote it, so it very well could be misleading on major legal theories. But it was a real exam answer which did very well (A), and was drafted using the class outline in Appendix 5. This is one answer of three in a three-hour exam period for a three-hour class focused on the issues of federal courts. This answer was worth 80 points in an exam totaling 180 points, and was expected to take 80 minutes of the three-hour exam period.*

As much as I would have liked to edit and correct this, I did not, in an attempt to provide an actual answer used on an actual exam. This exam was a time-crunch exam, and it became a race to finish. You will become familiar with different types of exams, one of which will be so long and full of so many issues that you immediately panic on seeing the exam questions. You literally will not set down your pencil for three hours, until time is called. The only comforting aspect of these exams is that everyone else is just as panicked and harried as you are, and hopefully you'll be able to pull yourself together better than they do.

My biggest complaint about the structure of my answer is that the introduction was sparse and I skipped a conclusion altogether. Although this didn't affect my grade as far as I can tell, strong beginnings and endings really help with the overall presentation of an answer.

This essay question ("fact pattern") focused on a man named Dan, a contractor for the federal government. He is being sued and is also suing various individuals.

Dan's alleged thriftiness has led to a complex chain of events requiring analysis of several issues. These issues will be addressed in turn.

I. Dan's Attempt to Enjoin Lucas

After Lucas sues Dan in state court, Dan files an action seeking an injunction from the federal court. The general rule under the Anti-Injunction Act (28 U.S.C. § 2283) is that a federal court cannot stay an ongoing proceeding in state court, with certain exceptions. The three exceptions to this rule are: if the injunction is "expressly authorized" (by statute), where an injunction is necessary in aid of jurisdiction, or to protect and effectuate a judgment. Working backward, the last exception won't fit this situation because there has been no previous federal judgment to protect. Likewise, the "in aid of jurisdiction" exception won't apply because this is not an "in rem" case (unless *somehow* employment can be considered "property"—but even then, the federal court didn't have the case first). So, we're left with the first exception—"expressly authorized." Under <u>Mitchum</u>, 42 U.S.C. § 1983 expressly authorizes injunctions against a state court. However, the <u>Younger</u> abstention doctrine will require the federal court to abstain unless there is evidence of bad faith, harassment, or other special circumstances. Assuming Dan could raise a § 1983 claim (although I'm not sure he can), or any other federal law which "expressly authorizes" injunctions, he would not be able to show any special circumstances that would allow a federal court to issue an injunction. Additionally, since Lucas' claim is a civil claim, there has to be an important state interest to justify application of <u>Younger</u>. It appears as if, on all counts, Dan should lose on his request for an injunction of Lucas' state law action.

II. Dan's Motion to Dismiss Lucas' Claims in Federal Court

Lucas has sued Dan in federal court for both a violation of the MPA and a <u>Bivens</u> action. Lucas is only entitled to a remedy under the MPA if it created a private federal right, and not merely a collective benefit. In order to find a private right (for which a remedy is available to an individual), the statute must include a clear indicator that it intends to create private rights for individuals. The biggest factor is the clear and unambiguous intent of Congress. While the MPA does assert that its purpose includes protecting individuals from retaliation, it also designed a remedial scheme to control contractor violations. When Congress creates a specific enforcement mechanism, there is enough evidence to imply that no private cause of action exists. Without clear language authorizing a suit by an employee against a private federal contractor, it will be difficult to find the existence of a private right purely under the MPA. Dan will most likely be successful on his motion to dismiss this claim.

Lucas, however, also has another action against Dan: a <u>Bivens</u> action. In order to prevail, Lucas' <u>Bivens</u> claim must show that a federal officer, under the color of federal law, intended to deprive him of a constitutional right (negligence will not suffice). This is like a § 1983 equivalent for federal officers. The unique limitation of a <u>Bivens</u> claim is that it will not be maintained if there are special factors counseling hesitation in the absence of affirmative steps by Congress, or Congress has provided an equal, alternative substitute.

Lucas' first potential problem occurs in showing the basic elements of a <u>Bivens</u> claim. In order for <u>Bivens</u> to apply, there must be state action (a private individual has no duty to observe the Constitutional rights of another); here, Lucas must show that Dan is a federal officer acting under color of federal law. While Dan is working for the government, he is a contractor. In <u>Malesko</u>, the Supreme Court held that a private entity cannot be subject to a <u>Bivens</u> action, but left open the question of individuals in employ with the private entity. Since individual officers within a private, contracted entity in a state can be held liable in their individual capacity under § 1983, there is a strong argument that Dan is a federal officer subject to a <u>Bivens</u> action. Assuming Dan is a federal official, and assuming Lucas has a constitutional claim, there could be special factors counseling hesitation (perhaps if this kind of claim is close enough to a suit arising under military service). Dan may also have a qualified immunity defense if his conduct did not violate clearly established statutory or constitutional rights—since this is a defense, however, it most likely won't be an issue in Dan's initial motion to dismiss. If the court finds a colorable constitutional claim, and finds Dan to be a federal officer, it should not dismiss his Bivens claim.

III. Dan's Request for Abstention

In the event the federal district court allows both of Lucas' claims against Dan to proceed, Dan has requested that it abstain. Since both of these claims involve a federal question, the federal district court has clear jurisdiction. Abstention doctrines are influenced by ideas of comity and are a way to protect an element of federalism. There are several types of abstention: Pullman, Burford, Thibedeaux, Colorado River, among others. Dan asserts that the state court should hear his state claim first, before the federal court takes the case. While the Pullman doctrine requires a federal court to abstain when there is an unsettled question of state law, which, when resolved, may eliminate the federal question, there is no evidence that the state law of wrongful discharge is unsettled here. Additionally, while the wrongful discharge is relevant, there is no indication that its resolution will eliminate the Constitutional question. There appears to be no administrative scheme to implicate Thibedeaux, and no concurrent/property issue to implicate Colorado River. Accordingly, Dan's request for abstention will most likely not be granted.

IV. Dan's Claim Against Brooke

Dan brought an action against Brooke in federal district court for violating/terminating his contract. The MPA provides that the oversight official (Brooke, in this case) can take remedial action not subject to federal court review. The question for the court to resolve is whether Congress has the power to restrict jurisdiction to exclude Dan's claim against Brooke. As a general rule, Congress can give less (but not more) jurisdiction to federal courts that the Constitution provides in Article 3. Article 3 provides for federal question jurisdiction, which Congress can restrict (and arguably, could possibly even eliminate). This restriction doesn't appear to violate the Constitution in and of itself (by violating Equal Protection, etc.). The only limit on restricting jurisdiction is that Congress can't take away all forums for a litigant. Assuming Dan can litigate his grievances another way in some manner, this restriction is an allowable act of Congress.

V. Supreme Court Review

Lucas is seeking Supreme Court review of his state supreme court's decision. Supreme Court review of state decisions is codified in 28 U.S.C. §1257. Generally, the Supreme Court can only review federal issues within a final judgment. There appears to be a final judgment on both claims, meaning there is to be no more litigation, or future litigation leaves no doubt as to the outcome (there is no more factual dispute).

On the issue of the correct statute of limitations, there appears to be no federal ingredient. The Supreme Court cannot review an issue of pure state law, and the state's decision will be final as to that.

On the second issue, the state supreme court interpreted a federal statute, the MPA. This raises a federal question which is reviewable by the Supreme Court. This would not have been prevented by the final judgment rule in Cox v. Cohn. However, since there are adequate and independent state law grounds, which are outcome determinative even if the MPA decision is reversed, the Supreme Court won't review any of Lucas' case (because, no matter what, it would still be banned because of the state statute of limitations). It seems as if the state decision will stand.

Acknowledgments

We would like to thank everyone who helped and supported us in writing this book. We wouldn't have been able to do this without our families and their endless support or without the scores of free editors who volunteered to read this for us, including our parents, Alison Durnavich, Tara Shaw, Catherine Boswell, César Cuauhtémoc García Hernández, Daniel May, Avery Sander, and Meg Myers Morgan. Thank you to Jim and Meg Morgan for indulging us with wonderful photographs. Carolina Academic Press took a chance on us, just a few faceless law students, and to them we are forever grateful.

We would also like to thank the professors and administrators who offered their advice, support, and encouragement: Lyn Entzeroth, Robert Spoo, Robert Butkin, Rex Zedalis, Marianne Blair, Kristine Bridges, Lauren Allison, Richard Ducey, and Raymond Yasser. And to our fellow students for agreeing to talk to us and giving us your input on the law school experience: **thank you.**